Sociology of Diversity series

Series Editor: **David G. Embrick**,
University of Connecticut, US

The Sociology of Diversity series brings together the highest quality
sociological and interdisciplinary research specific to ethnic, racial, gender
and sexualities diversities.

Forthcoming in the series:

Race, Diversity and Humanitarian Aid
Black Ecologies and the Problem of Whiteness in New Orleans
Diana Harvey

Out now in the series:

Disproportionate Minority Contact and Racism in the US
How We Failed Children of Color
Paul R. Ketchum and **B. Mitchell Peck**

Southern Craft Food Diversity
Challenging the Myth of a US Food Revival
Kaitland M. Byrd

Beer and Racism
How Beer Became White, Why It Matters, and the Movements to Change It
Nathaniel Chapman and **David Brunsma**

The Death of Affirmative Action?
Racialized Framing and the Fight Against Racial Preference in College Admissions
J. Scott Carter and **Cameron Lippard**

Find out more at

bristoluniversitypress.co.uk/sociology-of-diversity

Sociology of Diversity series

Series Editor: **David G. Embrick**,
University of Connecticut, US

Find out more at
bristoluniversitypress.co.uk/sociology-of-diversity

RACIAL DIVERSITY IN CONTEMPORARY FRANCE

The Case of Colorblindness

Marie des Neiges Léonard

BRISTOL UNIVERSITY PRESS

First published in Great Britain in 2022 by

Bristol University Press
University of Bristol
1-9 Old Park Hill
Bristol
BS2 8BB
UK
t: +44 (0)117 374 6645
e: bup-info@bristol.ac.uk

Details of international sales and distribution partners are available at bristoluniversitypress.co.uk

British Library Cataloguing in Publication Data
A catalogue record for this book is available from the British Library

ISBN 978-1-5292-0799-6 hardcover
ISBN 978-1-5292-0803-0 ePub
ISBN 978-1-5292-0802-3 ePdf

Cover design: blu inc
Front cover image: Unsplash/Thomas Deluzeh
Bristol University Press use environmentally responsible print partners.
Printed in Great Britain by CPI Group (UK) Ltd, Croydon, CR0 4YY

FSC
www.fsc.org
MIX
Paper from
responsible sources
FSC® C013604

To my father, Robert Léonard

To my daughter, Héloyse Léonard-Saillant

Contents

Series Editor Preface

I write this series editor preface from my hotel in Barcelona, Spain, just off Diagonal. I write this as several heartbreaking historical moments have come to pass – the US Supreme Court's reversing of *Roe v Wade*, for example, is just one of such moments. I wonder how much is too much. How many rights we are collectively willing to lose before enough is enough, before we finally decide to collectively galvanize our energies to push forward? Barcelona is interesting. In the time I have been here I have learned much about the municipalism movement that has been making great strides against neoliberalism, particularly privatization of public goods and spaces. It is refreshing to see community activism pushing back against the big banks, corporatism, and the long arm of capitalism. At the same time, while researching white spaces at the Museo Nacional d'Art de Catalunya, it has become more than apparent that racism, while openly dismissed or reduced to class issues like many countries in across the globe, is alive and well. Most prevalent, if you pay close attention, is anti-Black racism. Black people are routinely ignored, mistreated, or excluded from place and space in Barcelona. Of course, racism is complicated by immigration, as I was reminded by one of the members of Barcelona en Comu, a community-led organization deeply involved with the municipalism movement here. While folx here are concerned with steady immigration to Barcelona and its impact on gentrification of neighborhoods and displacement of residents, immigration has also become another code word for African or Black and is often used to promote exclusionary policies against folx classified as such.

It is with these thoughts in mind that I give further reflection to racism, and specifically anti-Black racism, in Europe. I note this with some clear caveats, fully understanding the complexities of Europe and the racist histories of the many countries that make up its mass, including those not part of the EU. The legacies of the transatlantic slavery and other racial atrocities aside, many European countries would recast themselves as post-racial or at least striving for some reckoning of their past. Hence, while we see instances of the concerning rise (or perhaps less fearful) of the far-right (see Corey Dolgon's book, *Kill It To Save It*, for a much more interesting take on this), most countries are more apt to take a more colorblind approach to issues of race and racism; there is a general disdain towards discussing race and racism (and even related language such as diversity) in many European countries.

In this, the fifth book published in the *Sociology of Diversity* series, titled *Racial Diversity in a Post-Racial World: The Case of Colorblindness in Contemporary France*, the author Marie des Neiges Léonard deftly interrogates diversity language in France, specifically the consequences of the new law eliminating the word "race" from the French Constitution. The author contends that the absence of racial categories in France in fact further exacerbates the underlying racism that continues to be pervasive in French society. In this book, Léonard not only does the job of dissecting how colorblind ideology partially informs how racism continues to operate systemically, but also explores how similar colorblind strategies are between France and the US, setting up a larger context from which to understand colorblind ideology at the global level. The timeliness of this book is striking, especially given the political discourse and backlash to race in both the US and across various countries in Europe.

David G. Embrick
University of Connecticut
Series Editor

List of Tables

About the Author

Marie des Neiges Léonard is a sociologist. She received her PhD in Sociology from Texas A&M University. Her research and teaching interests include race and gender, including comparative studies between the United States and European societies. She has published numerous essays on the question of race in France. Her scholarship on the question of race as a socially constructed category central to the debates in France demonstrates the natural progression of the author's expertise and research. She is currently teaching at the University of South Alabama, US.

Acknowledgments

This book would not have been possible without the constant and unwavering encouragement, support, patience, and mentorship of David G. Embrick, who has helped guide me through the trials and tribulations of the writing and publishing process. I am forever grateful to him for inviting me to be a contributing author and for pushing me, with firm kindness, to put together my manuscript. I would also like to acknowledge and thank him for providing me with pertinent and critical insights to improve and strengthen this book project.

Introduction

One would be hard pressed to find a section called "race" or "race and ethnicity" in a public library in France, the very country that has witnessed the development of modern sociology, from the works of Emile Durkheim to Pierre Bourdieu. In fact, the classification closest to "race" in the sociology section of a library would be "immigration," a combination of "immigration and integration," or, more rarely, "racism." Yet, on the other hand, in 2019, French television produced a successful drama mini-series, *Les Sauvages* (Savages), set in contemporary times, where the main character is a Kabyle-French man freshly elected president of France, that deals with issues such as prejudice and the trauma of French colonization and depicts what has been called a "multicultural France" or the "ethnic diversity of France" (Leblanc, 2019). In the first episode, the main character, Idder Chaouch, the newly elected French president (played by French-Moroccan actor Roschdy Zem), refers to "the colonial fact with its unsaid that's poisoning us, these truths that have been silenced so much that they have become lethal." And yet, race as a social category has not been referred to explicitly in the reviews of the program in French newspapers and magazines, which instead use the euphemism of a "young generation from immigrant background" to describe the characters.

American cultural critic and essayist Thomas Chatterton Williams, who works and lives in France, has been a vocal proponent of the idea of "retiring from race" and supports the idea of a post-racial society, an argument that has been praised in the French media. In his book *Self-Portrait in Black and White* (2019), Williams suggests "transcending" and "unlearning" race. In a February 2021 article in French national newspaper *Le Figaro*, Williams warns France against the American "obsession" with race and says he is more attached to the French model of citizenship without race. By refusing to focus obsessively on race, he believes that France allows its citizens a freedom that Americans don't have. Such statements have been echoed by French intellectuals and politicians.

Yet, as Jean Beaman (2018) explains in her essay on French Martinique-born political philosopher Frantz Fanon, although French identity is presented as nonracial and colorblind, Blackness is overdetermined from without the person and is also constitutive of a person's identity. In fact, for Beaman (2021), race remains a "never-ending taboo in France," since France is both "antiracial" in that it rejects racial terms and "nonracial" to the extent that it denies the social reality of race.

The purpose of this book is to broaden the discussion with regard to the taboo surrounding race and racial diversity in France, closely examining the paradox that France is a de facto multicultural society that nevertheless rejects multicultural practices and policies. One of the book's main aims is to challenge the notion that the French republican model is colorblind, as it seeks to present itself, and that it cannot therefore be racist because of its commitment to a form of colorblind legal equality.

More specifically, the goals of this book are threefold: (1) to interrogate the absence of racial categories in France, the different levels of denial surrounding this absence, the reasons for the taboo, and the debates that this absence and denials have provoked within French academia and in French society at-large; (2) to examine closely the debates and controversies about and around the question of race in contemporary France, because the way politicians and scholars engage in such debates, and what they choose or refuse to engage with, tells us as much as the content of the debates themselves; and (3) to show how an examination of the French case of colorblindness can help us make sense of colorblind racism not just as something specific to French society but as an example of what takes place in a colorblind society. Through this study, we learn how colorblind racism not only emerges, persists, and endures but also flourishes precisely because of and thanks to the colorblind form of equality at the heart of the French model.

The book examines these debates and issues through the lens of French and American theoretical paradigms in an attempt to make sense of the absence in official discourses of one of the most present and defining elements structuring French society.

Drawing in particular on the theoretical frameworks of American sociologists Joe Feagin (White racial frame), Eduardo Bonilla-Silva (colorblind racism), and Jennifer C. Mueller (racial ignorance), the book aims to uncover the strategies and repertoires used by different institutions of French society that help maintain the illusion of colorblindness, thus reinforcing colorblind racism itself.

Throughout the different chapters, the book will explore and examine different colorblind strategies, including: (1) the denial that race exists as a central structuring component of French social life; (2) a refusal to use racial categories in the French census, despite strong support from French sociologists and demographers to do so in order to collect accurate data; (3) the use of proxies or euphemisms instead of racial and ethnic terms; (4) the minimization or denial of the role ethnicity or race plays in discrimination patterns and instead claiming other nonracial factors (socioeconomic) may cause it; (5) the reluctance of institutions and policies to focus on race even while fighting systemic racism.

The book will also present and analyze the repertoires that provide nonracial justifications for the current colorblind social order in contemporary France, including:

1. French republicanism, often framed as neutral notion resting on the French Revolution's normative principles of "liberty, equality, fraternity," which acts as a gatekeeper to French citizenship;
2. abstract universalism and its ideals, also framed as the legacy of French republicanism, the French Revolution, and Enlightenment philosophy, according to which French society is governed by universal principles incompatible with race-conscious approaches like multiculturalism;
3. *laïcité* and the separation of church and state, a moral framework that defines French identity and has served as a frame of reference to evaluate issues such as the Islamic headscarf as well as freedom of speech and gender rights with regard to religion.

Finally, this book will introduce a new concept to help understand the French context in which colorblind ideologies emerged and are maintained. More specifically, the form of colorblind racism examined in the French case uses frameworks and language from the French Enlightenment to support racist ideologies, which, I contend, makes it an "enlightened racism."

As the book will show, what I call enlightened racism is an ideology that, first, relies on fantasized ideals of the French Revolution and the Enlightenment, such as universalism and *laïcité*; second, asserts that the ideals and principles that emerged from the French Revolution are race-neutral in their essence and solely based on citizenship; and third, claims it is not based on bigotry, or a lack of education, or a personal phobia but is instead based on an intellectually elaborate frame of argument that uses Enlightenment philosophical principles as a normative discourse and narrative to interpret reality. In turn, this normative discourse is used as an explanation either to defend personal racist attitudes or to justify racist institutional policies.

The premise of the debate: colorblind and post-racial

As argued by Patrick Simon (2017: 2330), "France stands out as the archetype of a colorblind society." In many ways and at different levels, it is as if France not only remains oblivious to the significance of race in its own history but

3

also chooses to ignore and deny it. France also chooses to reject and attack any ideas, theories, and actions coming from political or academic circles that might study, examine, and promote analysis of and policies toward racial inequalities in France. The reemergence of the word race in current French public discourse seems to operate as a sort of magical thought, consisting of either silencing a word with the intent to eliminate the reality to which it refers, or, on the contrary, tirelessly pronouncing it in order to exorcize it.

In September 2019, in the French political and news weekly magazine *Le Point* (September 13, 2019), 80 French intellectuals – including Alain Finkielkraut, Elisabeth Badinter, Jean-Pierre Le Goff, Mona Ozouf, and Pierre Nora – signed a call against other French intellectuals, identified as belonging to a movement defending a "decolonization" of thought, of the arts, and so on.

The movement to which these 80 French intellectuals refer is composed of: Le Parti des Indigènes de la République, Collectif contre l'islamophobie en France, Marche des femmes pour la dignité, Marches de la dignité, Camp décolonial, Conseil représentatif des associations noires, Conseil représentatif des Français d'outre-mer, Brigade antinégrophobie, Décoloniser les arts, Les Indivisibles (Rokhaya Diallo), Front de mères, collectif MWASI, collectif Non MiXte.s racisé.e.s, Boycott désinvestissement sanctions, Coordination contre le racisme et l'islamophobie, Mamans toutes égales, Cercle des enseignant.e.s laïques, Les Irrécupérables, and Réseau classe/genre/race, among others. While all fight for social justice, each of these collective organizations have their own goals and missions: some are focused on antiracism, some aim to end systemic violence against women of color, some target patriarchy and capitalism, some are purposefully non-mixed (for women of color-only, for example), and some seek to combat discrimination against Muslims in France.

The "call of the 80" warns against what they see as a dangerous shift by this group of movements and school of thought toward "reactivating" the notion of race, which the 80 intellectuals see as a negative development. The 80 intellectuals from the fields of postcolonial, gender, and racial studies accuse those promoting this shift of being academic imposters who are trying "to make their ideologies pass as if they were scientific truth," and to serve their own interests to the detriment of republican universalism. The call of the 80 even goes as far as describing the strategy of the "combat activists" of the "decolonize" movement as intellectual terrorism, comparing their behavior to Stalinism. To these 80 intellectuals, the "situation is alarming" because they claim that members of the "decolonize" movement are using the strategy of entryism within higher education and the culture industry to take over academia, among other things. They also view the "decolonize" movement's focus on "state racism" as an attack on universalism, as well as the foundational principles of the French Republic – "liberty, equality, fraternity."

In the newspaper *Le Parisien* (March 24, 2021), Olivier Faure, leader of the French Socialist Party, declared "our DNA is republican, universalist, and secular" in response to a student union that held a meeting exclusively open to students of color. Faure views these student meetings as manifesting a problematic drift toward a "secessionist project" within French society. Faure also claims that when such events — that is, "non-mixed racialized" meetings — take place, a line is crossed because their very occurrence tends to promote what he describes as an essentialization of individuals, which in turn challenges the principle of French "universalism (then) condemned and presented as an ideology of domination for the White Western society" (*Le Parisien*, March 24, 2021). Faure and other French politicians thus view such movements that challenge the French universalist principle as unacceptable and believe that they should be shut down.

In addition to allowing us to unpack the idea of colorblindness, the French context also raises the question of the salience of the notion of a post-racial society, since on the surface it seems that French society is colorblind and is thus something of a poster country for a post-racial world. The term "post-racial" was first used in the United States, without really being defined, by journalists in the fall of 2008 to describe a situation in which, if Senator Barack Obama was elected, the topic of race would become irrelevant by the very fact that a Black man had been elected to the country's highest political office (Gillespie, 2009). Obama's ascent to the White House in 2008 was applauded by countless people around the world as an unprecedented success story not just for racial minorities in the United States but for minorities worldwide. Indeed, the implication of Obama's election was that racial equality had finally been achieved, and that therefore racial differences or even racial identities were no longer significant. A new and improved America had emerged in which the primacy of racial identities had finally melted and transcended into a true pluralistic nation (see, for example, Joe Klein's article in *Time Magazine*, November 5, 2008, headlined "Obama's victory ushers in a New America").

Analyzing the implications of Obama's election as president of the United States, American historian David A. Hollinger defines a post-racial world as

> a possible future in which the ethnoracial categories central to identity politics would be more matters of choice than ascription; in which mobilization by ethnoracial groups would be more a strategic option than a presumed destiny attendant upon mere membership in a group; and in which economic inequalities would be confronted head-on, instead of through the medium of ethnorace. (Hollinger, 2008: 1033)

In fact, Hollinger (2011) views ethno-racial systems (such those that make use of racial identity and racial categories) as "increasingly anachronistic" and advocates for a move from the problem of the color line (as had American sociologist W. E. B. Du Bois, who in 1903 declared this to be the main problem of the 20th century) to the problem of solidarity, where "color-coded races" are considered an artifact with which people choose whether and how much they wish to affiliate, rather than an imposed, deterministic category.

The foreign press talked about this "new," supposedly post-racial America as a victory over racism. For example, when Obama was elected, German newspapers *Berliner Morgenpost* and *Bild* described him as the "new" or "black" Kennedy. On November 5, 2008, French newspaper *Le Figaro* cheered for "The New America" while French newspaper *Le Monde* proclaimed: "First we must write these words. Read them slowly out loud to take measure of the scale of the event, its emotional and historical charge: The American people have just elected, in the White House, a man with a black skin." Most of the European press at the time portrayed Obama as a symbol of change, and they did so from a racial perspective by describing him as a multicultural president. As Rama Yade (then Secretary of State for Human Rights in the French government) declared: "This is the fall of the Berlin Wall times ten" (Poggioli, 2009a). After the US election, Patrick Lozès (founder and president of the Conseil Représentatif des Associations Noires de France, a grassroots umbrella organization for Black associations in France) noted that "what's so extraordinary about Barack Obama's election is that this was the first time we didn't hear only negative things about us." He also added that "young people now believe they can conquer the world ... A black can be an ambassador, a doctor, anything" (Poggioli, 2009b). In other words, Obama's election demonstrated that being a minority does not lock someone into a preset position or low status in society. It gave minorities a new sense of self-belief about what is achievable.

This "miracle," as it was sometimes called in the European press, motivated Yazid Sabeg (an Arab French businessman serving as Commissioner for Diversity and Equality of Chances, a position attached to the Cabinet of the Prime Minister in France) to launch "A Manifesto for Real Equality. Yes, We Can!," which was published in a weekly French newspaper (*Le Journal du Dimanche*, 2008). In it, Sabeg writes: "America has confirmed the validity of a democratic model founded on equity and diversity; and therefore it's no surprise that Obama is so popular in France, his popularity demonstrates the aspirations of all the children of the Republic." Sabeg also urged the French government to adopt policies equivalent to that of affirmative action. "Positive actions," as Sabeg calls them, have enabled "the black middle class to emerge."

Following Obama's election and reelection in 2008 and 2012, parts of the European media claimed that it seemed as if America and American politics had successfully transcended race, thus ushering in an era of post-racial politics. This post-racial idea quickly became a dominant theme in European politics and found a particularly strong echo in France, as if to confirm the validity and legitimacy of a colorblind approach and ideology.

Book structure

The book is divided into six chapters.

Chapter 2 provides some foundational definitions with regard to race and racism, according to current sociological approaches. The chapter also offers some important points of reference in terms of the history and significance of the word race in the French context, as well as the use of race and racism as part of the French colonial project. The chapter then introduces the theoretical frameworks that will be used to examine colorblind racism patterns in France and presents the debates that have taken place among French scholars over the lack of racial statistics in the census.

Chapter 3 explores the contemporary demography of France, underlining the issues that French scholars face when trying to provide an accurate account of the diversity of the French population in the absence of racial statistics. The chapter also presents the antidiscrimination and diversity structures and legal system currently in place in France before turning to the existing patterns of racial discrimination and racism in different sectors and institutions of French society, namely employment, education, housing, health, and the police.

Chapter 4 critically reviews the existing census and data collection methods in France, pointing to the contradictions and paradoxes related to a colorblind system that denies the presence of racial categories on the one hand while using proxies to account for the diversity of identities among its residents on the other. It also offers some comparative analysis with how other countries in Europe handle the census count of their racial minorities.

Chapter 5 relates and describes the 2005 riots that took place in the French *banlieues* (suburbs) as well as their aftermath. It also presents the different approaches that have previously been used to examine the riots and offers an alternative analysis by applying Bonilla-Silva's concept of colorblind racism and Feagin's notion of the White racial frame to the French context. It then discusses the ideas behind the French model of integration, highlighting its inadequacies in recognizing the issues of discrimination and systemic racism that French minorities face on a daily basis.

Chapter 6 focuses on the presence of Islam in France, the country's second religion after Catholicism. It first presents the demographics of the Muslim population in France, noting that due to data collection limitations, numbers may misrepresent a more diverse reality. This chapter also offers an analysis of the ongoing issue of the Islamic veil in terms of the racial framing of Islam through the narratives of *laïcité*, universalist feminism, and the republican idea of free speech, focusing on the negative consequences for Muslim women in France. Finally, the chapter reviews the legal systems in place in other European countries compared with the French regulations.

Chapter 7 provides some concluding remarks and summarizes the book's main findings with regard to the idea of contemporary France as a model of presumed colorblindness and the denial of race and racial categories perpetuated in French society. It also proposes recommendations for public policy and possible new approaches in creating a more race-conscious society, going beyond the French exception.

This book is not a final or definitive account of France's case; it is instead a snapshot of a continuously evolving dynamic that involves micro and macro processes, which have both ideological and practical implications for the lives of the individuals impacted by such systems.

2

Race and Racism:
Framing the Debate

In France, race and the discussion of race in public debates and in the social sciences have been treated as offshore or off-limits, and at best as a euphemism. This book intends to shed some light on the debates and controversies about France's blind spot as well as to unveil the profound reasons for the country's refusal to recognize race.

Eliminating the word "race" from the French Constitution was a campaign promise made by François Hollande in 2012, an aim supported by League Internationale Contre le Racisme et l'Antisémitisme (LICRA, International League Against Racism and Anti-Semitism) President Mario Stasi, who declared that the presence of the word in Article 1 of the French Constitution represented a "dangerous archaism" (*Le Monde*, June 26, 2018). On July 12, 2018, the representatives of the French National Assembly voted unanimously to eliminate the word from the Constitution.

Fast forward to 2020. During his speech on June 10 addressing the question of racism and discrimination, President Emmanuel Macron stated that racism was a "disease that touches all of society" and described racism and discrimination as a "plague that is a betrayal of the republican universalism" (*Le Monde*, June 10, 2020). It was as though he was saying that universalism is a rampart against racism but that it had fallen under a viral attack, similar perhaps to that of the COVID-19 pandemic, and also opposing universalism and race, which will be discussed later in the chapter.

And yet, presently, the first article of the French Constitution still reads:

> France is a Republic, indivisible, secular, democratic and social. It ensures equality before the law of all its citizens without any distinction of origin, race, or religion. It respects all the beliefs. Its organization is decentralized. The law also encourages equal access to women and men to electoral mandates and functions, as well as to professional and social responsibilities.

Here, the French Constitution names race only to outlaw it. The concept of race appears with the sole purpose of immediately denying it of any existence or significance. That race should not be a relevant factor of distinction in terms of legal rights for all citizens of France is clear and makes sense for a society that promotes and defends equality. What is problematic is the denial, through the desire of elimination, of the significant role that race plays in the social life of French citizens, as if to say that by the simple virtue of enunciating the non-significance of race, the law eliminates its existence. But how, then, can the Constitution announce that race will have no relevance without first acknowledging its existence and without defining what the term implies?

Although French society wishes to depict itself as a colorblind society, as exemplified by this act of elimination from the highest legal document in France, the French Republic is anything but. From the different governmental agencies investigating racial discrimination to ethnic riots placing the fate of racial minorities residing in the Parisian *banlieues* and elsewhere at the forefront of the news and of discussions about the French republican model, to debates among French scholars about the possibility of using ethnic statistics for social science research, or simply regarding the existence of postcolonial studies departments in French universities, the question of race is at the center, not the margins, of French society. French society may present itself as – or may wish to be – colorblind, when in fact, race may very well be its blind spot. It is in this context that my work came to the fore. It is precisely because race is out of frame, one might say "out of sight out of mind," a central operative concept in French society yet nonexistent in official classifications, that I intend to examine this denial of the repressed.

This chapter will first introduce and define the terms central to the analysis of this book, namely race and racism as well as racial identity and racial identity politics. It will then review the history of race in France, including the links between race, colonialism, and slavery. Finally, the chapter presents the main theoretical frames relevant to the study of race and racial diversity in the 21st century, with a particular focus on the works of Feagin and Bonilla-Silva, as a way to examine the French case through the lens of American theory. The chapter will also engage with the works of French scholars and expose the main contradictions and questions arising from past and current debates among them, and political actors as well, with regard to race and racism in France.

Race: some definitions

For the purpose of the topic and focus of this book, I use multiple approaches to define race.

A basic starting point could be that race refers to physical differences that groups and cultures consider socially significant. Dorothy Roberts (2012: 5) explains that race is a "political category" and a "political system" (in Golash-Boza, 2016). Tanya Golash-Boza (2016) argues that a definition of race must also include a definition of racism, as the construction of racial categories has historically been connected to the construction and reproduction of racism. Similarly, Amanda Lewis (2004: 625) contends that "*race* as a set of identities, discursive practices, cultural forms, and ideological manifestations would not exist without racism." Race, therefore, can be defined as a master status that involves beliefs, practices, and ideologies about the racial identity of individuals. There is seldom disagreement among social scientists that race is a socially constructed category. The common understanding is that race is not biologically relevant but is socially significant. In other words, we may think that the human race is one and indivisible biologically, but while race, like other social categories such as class and gender, is a socially constructed category that does not contain any biological foundation, it still has a social reality. It is more than just an idea. Once the idea of race is constructed, it produces real effects on the political and social actors (Bonilla-Silva, 2006: 9) and has ramifications in legal, political, economic, and structural terms because the idea of race establishes a relationship of correlation between a physical element (skin color) and intellectual and moral qualities. The discursive processes that construct racial categories are not immune from political implications; not only do these processes accompany actions but they are, already, acts themselves.

Taking these considerations into account, we could define race in several ways. It is a socially constructed division between humans based on presumed essential, natural, or culturally distinctive characteristics that are assumed to be linked. Race is also a historico-ideological construction manifesting itself through its performativity, in other words, a reality that it creates by inducing a model of social relations based on hierarchies within which individuals move. Finally, race can be analyzed as the incarnation of a normative process that constitutes a matrix of identity that the racialized subject still has room to subvert and transgress (Donnet et al, 2010). According to this definition, racial classifications thus imply a hierarchy where members of the different groups are classified in inferior or superior rankings, physically, culturally, psychologically, morally, and aesthetically, according to their attributed race. As Golash-Boza (2016) argues, we cannot separate the construction of race from the reproduction of racism.

Conceptualizing racism

From a conceptual standpoint, most race scholars agree that racism forms a structure (Bonilla-Silva) or is systemic (Feagin).

For French social scientist Magali Bessone, the question of defining racism includes resolving the issue of the relationship between the racist structure and the racist individual. According to Bessone (2017), racism in its cognitive aspect comprises beliefs and judgments organized together in narratives that interpret reality and transpose themselves into individual practices of exclusion, or into unequal institutional structures. The content of these narratives focuses on an essentialization and naturalization of differences that can be observed between groups in order to justify a hierarchical classification of human beings. The ideological content of racism relies on a double assertion: first that race is a category of essential, natural, or cultural divisions between human beings; and second that the hierarchy between each socially constructed race is affirmed through a classification of their members, who are seen as physically, culturally, mentally, morally, and aesthetically inferior in virtue of their assumed race.

These two ideological statements are used to justify the unequal political, economic, and social treatment of groups that are different from the dominant group. Thus, racism is a process of hierarchization of difference based on race – whatever the racial markers, skin color or otherwise – that legitimizes the exploitation, oppression, and unequal treatment of others. Furthermore, a racist ideology is always institutionalized. It doesn't matter that the science demonstrates the invalidity of the arbitrary classifications – racism does not disappear because it is institutionalized.

But racism is multisite, with multiple locations: it is a judgment, a structure, and a psycho-physiological disposition. For Bessone (2017), racism is, fundamentally, a complex moral disposition; it is also an ideology that refers to a more or less organized group of representations reflecting a deformed relationship with reality based on erroneous theories that are nonetheless viewed as valid and self-evident. It is also a moral disposition with an expressive dimension, specific to the lack of respect toward individuals or groups who are racialized. Racism is located within individuals and within structures.

The work of sociologists examining racism is precisely to situate the different locations of racism in order to resolve the question of the relationship between the racist individual and the racist structure, analyze it, and determine the most efficient public policies to fight against it.

Racism's ideological content involves two assertions:

1. that race is a category of essential divisions, cultural or natural, between humans, which implies bio-behavioral essences; and
2. that there is a hierarchy of races, in which individuals are ranked physically, aesthetically, morally, mentally, and culturally inferior due to their presupposed racial membership.

These two assertions serve as justifications for the inequality in the social, economic, and political treatment of different groups. In that sense, racist ideology is institutionalized, because, despite scientific demonstrations from ethnology, anthropology, genetics, phylogenetics, and empirical data that races don't exist biologically, and that any biological classification is erroneous, racism still exists. So it is not about knowledge. And it isn't an error of judgment; nor is it a cognitive dysfunction.

A combination of Michel Wieviorka's (1998) approach and W. Carson Byrd's (2011) perspective will also inform my definition of racism. For French historian Wieviorka, racism involves "characterizing a human group with natural attributes that are themselves connected with intellectual and moral qualities …, and from there eventually putting in place a process of inferiorization and exclusion practices" (1998: 7). Byrd (2011) claims that while it may seem simple to identify the purpose of racism (racial oppression, racial exploitation), defining what racism is and how it operates is not. For Byrd, one such possible definition is that racism is a "multilevel system of oppression based on the social categories of race whereby the subordinate group subordinates members of other racial groups using overt and covert methods among the individuals, institutions, organizations, and patterns of interactions in society" (2011: 1008).

Martin Reisigl and Ruth Wodak (2015) add that racism contains practices and processes that involve naturalizing and generalizing cultural differences and social construction as well as hierarchies. Specifically:

> Natural and cultural differences are marked and stereotypically generalized and polarized to construct homogeneous groups or communities of persons.
>
> These two types of differences are connected via the naturalization of cultural differences. This implies that fictitious or real, usually visible, more or less unchangeable features are linked - as allegedly natural traits - with social, cultural, or mental characteristics (naturalization of cultural differences).
>
> This naturalizing social construction is accompanied by the hierarchization and negative evaluation of the racialized "other."
>
> Naturalized hierarchization and negative evaluation serve to justify and legitimize power differences, exploitation, and social and political exclusion. (Reisigl and Wodak, 2015: 578)

Finally, Golash-Boza (2015) defines racism as the "ideology that races are populations of people whose physical differences are linked to significant cultural and social differences, and that these innate hierarchical differences can be measured and judged," as well as "the micro and macrolevel practices that subordinate those races believed to be inferior" (Golash-Boza, 2015).

The history of race and racism in France

If the word race has no biological reality, it nevertheless refers to a historical and social reality. Despite the race-neutral or colorblind approach that the French state promotes, notably through the absence of racial statistics in the census, French history has not been inherently colorblind. As argued by Erik Bleich (2000), public discussions about race and racism in France often overlook the long experience of the French state with colonies and mass slavery, which included racial and racist policies. However, racial and ethnic consciousness and discourse were not restricted to the colonial context. We must also examine other periods of French history showing race-conscious ideas and ideologies, as this will allow us to better grasp the complexity of the French experience with race and understand current political choices with regard to race.

The word "race" first appeared in the French vocabulary around the 1500s. At that time, it first and foremost related to notions of family, ascendance, descendance, genealogy, and generation, and was hence at the same level of blood and descent ("souche," or root/stock). It is in this sense that classical French authors used the term (for example, in the 17th century, Pierre Corneille, Jean Racine). At that point, the obsession with purity was such that the word race was used to distinguish aristocrats from those who were not part of the aristocracy. Nobles claimed their race as the heredity basis of their value and status (the physical and mental strength necessary to carry a sword, for example), and by opposition, the word race did not apply to commoners. In the early 18th century, Henri de Boulainvilliers (1727) provided a formal theory justifying the status of the privileged by awarding them a different racial origin from that of the commoners, thereby presenting the nobles as the heirs of the German conquerors.

In the early to mid-19th century, many French thinkers and historians (for example, Augustin Thierry, Jules Michelet) who were attached to the newly founded republican principles (liberty, equality, fraternity), reversed the former hierarchy where race was the mark of the aristocratic cast while still maintaining the principle of racial differences. More specifically, such thinkers argued that the "Gaul race embodies equality and the German race the aristocracy." The rationale for such a claim lies in the contradictions between the universalist principle of the 1789 French Revolution and the desire to maintain a reference to ethnic oppositions. The blood of the ancestors as a proxy for race thus helped provide significance to original divisions. Bleich (2000) also argues that the theorizing of race and racist ideas was generally well developed from the 18th to the 20th century in French thought, for example among renowned intellectuals such as Georges-Louis Leclerc de Buffon, Arthur de Gobineau, Hippolyte Taine, and Ernest Renan.

Starting in the late 1600s, and further again in the 19th century, the categorization of differences using race as a marker was expressed in a new context, that of colonialism and slavery.

Colonization and slavery are indeed the most important economic phenomenon, quantitatively speaking (in terms of the number of men and women being exploited, and the volume of commercial production and exchange), of Western history from the 16th to the 19th centuries. Starting in the late 1600s, as explained by Sue Peabody (1994), France expanded its trade through colonization and slavery. As an ideology supporting the colonial enterprise and slave trade, and thus, as a system, racism constructed races as the easiest, most superficial, most arbitrary, but also the most convenient distinction between humans for colonizers. More specifically, as Odile Tobner (2007: 78) writes, skin color was "elevated to the rank of metaphysics of humankind."

In some ways, as Colette Guillaumin wrote in the 1970s, followed by Véronique De Rudder in the 1990s (Matas and Pfefferkorn, 2010), it is "racism that precedes race, invents it, and makes it exist socially" (De Rudder, 1996). It is the reality of racism that makes race real, not the other way around. In this sense, race is not a preliminary or prerequisite to the racialization of society but its product. Peabody (2004) does not see antiBlack racism as an accidental cultural construct originating from slavery. Rather, based on historical accounts, she demonstrates that antiBlack racism was based on an already existing body of archived images that colonizers could use and apply to their own ends as a justification for conquest, occupation, and exploitation. For example, she shows that the construction of "race-thinking" or race-consciousness can be traced to early French missionaries' writings and their attention to color, their negative stereotyping of Black people, and their justification of the enslavement, which they link to skin color as a mark of enslavement (Peabody, 2004). Thus, negative images of Black people were available to colonizers from the outset, enabling them to adopt and adapt them to meet their moral, legal, and/or religious justifications for conquest. The dominant system's ideological justifications simply changed according to the needs and contexts. In any case, historians show that starting in the late 16th century, the notion of epidermalization, a term coined by Fanon and defined here as the process by which perception of color entraps the racialized body within its skin, became a central feature of French society. In a 1654 book, Jean-Baptiste Du Tertre (a Dominican priest who participated in the French colonization of the Antilles) examines the etymology of the word mulatto, which he defines as: "children ... engendered from a white man and a black woman, much like the mule is the product of two animals from different species" (Du Tertre, 1654).

Several pieces of legislation have been key in the construction of race thinking and of a racial ideology justifying the actions of the French colonial power.

If the *Six Livres de la République* of Jean Bodin (1576) only mentions the status of slaves on French soil, declaring that "any slave who sets foot on French soil is free," the text does not refer to the question of race or skin color.

However, the "Code Noir" (Black Code), a 1685 decree issued by Louis XIV addressing the conditions of Black slaves in the French colonial empire (notably America and the French Antilles at the time), specifically refers to Black people and the idea of race. From its title, this legal document directly and openly includes the identification and association between skin color (Black) and status (slave). Among other things, the decree aimed to give a legal and institutional frame – and hence legitimacy – to the trade in slaves, restricting their status and activities. For example, it is specified that Black slaves, which the decree calls "Negroes," are to be considered "personal property," with all the attendant legal consequences and ramifications. Through the law, the Code Noir established that Black slaves had no legal rights as individuals, as persons, as humans. According to Tobner (2007: 84), the "ferocity of the Code Noir betrays the fear of rebellion and escape" of slaves from their White masters. The code was also a way to legitimize, formally, the oppression and exploitation of slaves and cancel and prevent any practice or treatment deemed too permissive toward Black slaves. This 17th-century code thus clearly and explicitly refers to the notion of race, linking skin color to sociopolitical status. Tyler Stovall (2006) argues that the Code Noir is "one of the most extensive official documents on race, slavery, and freedom ever drawn up in Europe."

An 18th-century piece of legislation, the Edict of October 1716, establishes "the conditions under which colonists could bring their slaves to France without losing them." In the late 17th and early 18th centuries, as Peabody (1994) notes, an increasing number of White slaveowners started to bring their Black slaves to France to work as domestic servants. The Mayor of the city of Nantes asked King Louis XIV to create a law addressing the status of slaves in France in order to counteract the previous 16th-century republican principle that "any slave who sets foot on French soil is free." The edict proclaimed by the King restricted the way that slaveowners could bring their slaves to France. The edict relies heavily on the 17th-century Code Noir, which legitimizes slavery as "necessary and authorized" and as a consequence implies that since a slave was legally owned by their owner, "merely stepping on French soil was not enough to free him," contrary to the 16th-century principle. The terminology refers to "Negro slaves" or simply "Negroes," as the two terms became interchangeable. Further, the Declaration of 1738, a revised version of the 1716 Edict, uses the terms "slave negroes," "negro slaves," and "negroes," which also became interchangeable, signifying that race and slave status are the same.

During that period of French Enlightenment, French philosopher Montesquieu (whose work is still studied in French schools) published his treatise of political theory (*The Spirit of the Laws*, 1748). Although he dedicates chapters to the question of slavery, he never mentions the Code Noir, which, as a legal scholar, he must have known about. Yet, not only does Montesquieu fail to cite, or still less critically analyze, the Code Noir, as he does with other pieces of legislation, he also provides reasons to support the right to "make negroes slaves": of the nine reasons he puts forward, two are based on economics, five on skin color, and two on religion and politics. Montesquieu also conceptualizes a theory of climate, establishing a link between climate and character, arguing that under hot climates, which weaken courage, men are only inclined to do hard work under the fear of punishment (*Esprit des Lois*, L. XV, chapter VII), hence justifying the recourse to slavery. Contemporary French scholars have seldom critically examined Montesquieu's work, with the exception of Aimé Césaire, who has noted a connection between Montesquieu's ideas and an early form of scientific racism (Tobner, 2007).

Similarly, in his *Treatise of Metaphysics* (1734), French philosopher Voltaire formulates the idea that "the race of negroes is a different kind of species than ours." In his *Essay on Universal History, the Manners, and Spirit of Nations* (1756), Voltaire argues that what he sees as a proof of stupidity by Black people ("a proof that negroes don't have common sense, is that they make a greater case of a glass necklace than gold, which, amongst civilized nations, is of great importance") is enough to justify slavery.

In both cases, what is noteworthy in Montesquieu's and Voltaire's works is the use of physical differences such as skin color and other characteristics as evidence for the existence of different biological races on a hierarchical scale, placing Black people at an inferior level to White people and thus serving as a justification for their enslavement. Regarding the role of philosophers of the Enlightenment period in France, Césaire (1939) wrote: "[I]f there was a general judgment to give about the behavior of politicians of the French Revolution regarding the colonial issue, perhaps we should say that nothing else was as foreign to them as was anticolonialism, and that the anti-colonial approach stayed at a sentimental level: philanthropy."

These laws were followed by the Code de l'Indigénat (also called régime de l'Indigénat, or simply Indigénat), a set of laws and regulations regarding the legal and penal status of native or indigenous people in the French colonies from 1881 to 1947. By 1887, decrees had been put in place throughout the entire French colonial empire in various ways. The code included several types of measures: requisitions of goods and lands, collective fines, imprisonment, forced labor, disciplinary sanctions. In essence, the regime imposed specific penalties for the *indigènes* and organized the seizure or appropriation of their lands, but it also applied repressive measures against indigenous people at the civil level, in terms of their personal status, and at the political level, with partial or nonexistent political rights. For example, they had limited voting rights: this meant that indigenous people did not have the right to vote in general or national elections in their own country, but only had legal access to voting for local elections and in Muslim organizations. In other words, indigenous people were not allowed to participate in the democratic process of their own country.

The Code de l'Indigénat distinguished two categories of citizens: French citizens with French ancestry from metropolitan France, and French subjects, that is, Black Africans, Malagasy, Algerians, Antilles, Melanesians, and so on. All French subjects who fell under the Code de l'Indigénat were denied most of the political liberties and rights that were given to French citizens. While all *indigènes* could in theory become citizens, the admission requirements were so difficult that only a small proportion of candidates were actually selected. Furthermore, even when an *indigène* converted to Christianity, they would continue to be counted in the category of "Muslim subject."

For French historian Emmanuelle Saada (2014), the notion of *indigène* in Algeria is very much racialized. Indeed, in 1874 Algeria's Court of Appeals stated that the "indigène expression includes … all individuals who live in the north of Africa and who do not belong to the European race." This was confirmed in 1903 by the Court of Cassation of Paris, which defined the expression as including "all indigènes of African race." Thus, very far removed from the principles of citizenship of the 1789 French Revolution, the Code de l'Indigénat views *indigènes* as French subjects without any of the rights of French citizens. Furthermore, Saada argues that in the "European Empires, the law was one of the instances of production of race" and that, "from the relative autonomy came a legal usage of race that mixed in an original way some biological elements with social and political considerations" (2014: 51).

During the Second World War, the "Loi du 3 Octobre 1940 portant statut des juifs" (Law of October 3, 1940 on the status of the Jews), also called "first status of Jews," was passed by the Vichy regime, providing a legal frame to the expression at the time "of Jewish race," which would be used during the Nazi occupation in order to implement racist and anti-Semitic policies. The law was applied in all of France but with additional decrees in the occupied zone of France. A police force was specially created in 1942 for the sole purpose of applying the Law of October 3, 1940. The law articulates two main points: the first is to define who will be considered of Jewish race, and the second is to establish and enforce legal discrimination against Jewish individuals. The decree of application of the law also gives a legal framework to individual arrests and massive raids, among which was the infamous Vel d'Hiv Roundup of July 16, 1942.

Debates and controversies

One of the questions raised by Didier Fassin and Patrick Simon (2008: 41) is how scholars can name a social reality without contributing to making it exist in reality. They also wonder, as a connected issue, whether classifying could become a way to create hierarchies.

These are questions that have been at the center of the debates that have divided French scholars into opposing camps since the late 1990s and the start of the 21st century without really finding a satisfactory resolution (De Rudder and Vourc'h, 2006).

In particular, Patrick Simon and Joan Stavo-Debauge (2004) talk about a controversy that erupted among demographers in France a year before the 1999 French Census over a rumored plan to include ethnic categories in the questionnaire (Simon, 2008a). In a previous population survey, French demographer Michèle Tribalat had used native language to distinguish among the diverse native African ethnic groups and introduced the concept of "ethnic belonging" in the analysis of the survey. Following this epistemological stance, a debate erupted between Tribalat and French historian Hervé Le Bras. The controversy opposed believers in a colorblind model (like Le Bras) that does not include any reference to race or ethnicity in the census (as it currently was and is), and challengers or taboo breakers (like Tribalat), who wanted to introduce new categories into the census, going beyond the nationality criteria. The media has presented this controversy as an opposition between "ethnicists" and "republicans" (defenders of the universal ideals of the French Republic). When the controversy ended, the status quo prevailed and resulted in even greater limitations on access to information about nationality or country of birth. French social scientists supporting a color-blind approach to demographic studies consider that racial categories are not useful scientifically and divisive ideologically, and thus they should not be added to demographic data. The controversy was particularly vitriolic because the stakes go beyond the question's simple scientific or technical aspects. It is not just an issue of analytical concept or principles but about transforming the way experts and individuals construct knowledge about their world and how they represent it.

The controversy resumed in 2004 (Simon, 2017) in a different political and social context where the topic of discrimination was now part of political debates and campaigns. During that time, two petitions from French social scientists with opposing standpoints were published in the French newspapers *Libération* and *Le Monde*. One petition ("Republican commitment against discrimination") argued that the fight against discrimination could be waged using currently available data and methods. The signatories also warned against the dangers of using "ethnical statistics" that would promote divisions among communities – notably through programs such as "positive discrimination," also known as affirmative action – and work against an inclusive, universalist republican model (*Libération*, February 23, 2007). In response, the sponsors of the other petition, among whom was the French demographer Patrick Simon, sought to bring attention to the inadequacies of the current statistical data for the examination of discrimination and the drafting of antidiscrimination policies. They also argued for the use of accurate statistics, including ethnic categories.

The difference in the second round of debates was that the stakes of the issue went beyond its epistemological and technical aspects and became a political battleground. Polemics ensued between the pro and con camps, and these arguments have since prevented the possibility of making any real headway into finding solutions, or at least alternatives. The four main arguments against the use of ethnic statistics are:

1. too many historical precedents have shown the dangers of the inappropriate use of ethnic records for political or other purposes, and thus society should avoid using racial categories;
2. the use of racial categories will essentialize individuals and promote stereotyping;
3. racial categories are too strict and rigid and do not accurately represent people's identities; and
4. ethnic statistics are not necessary to fight discrimination, which can be revealed through other data and methods already in place.

The debates over the collection of ethnic statistics in France is a reflection of the degree of confusion "regarding both the kind of statistics that one is talking about and the purpose(s)" the statistics are supposed to achieve (Sabbagh and Peer, 2008). The only concept mentioned in the debates is "ethnicity" or ethnic categories, not race. And so, for example, the debate has been presented in terms of "ethnic statistics" rather than racial statistics or statistics that would include race. In fact, explains François Héran, legal scholars have used the words ethnic and racial as synonyms, when, as he notes, "anthropologists don't accept that." Along with the categories of immigrants, foreigners, French by birth, and French by acquisition of nationality, there is an underlying category that social scientists use: "majority population," which is defined as "all the French that are not immigrants or sons or daughters of immigrants or of persons born in the French overseas departments" (Beauchemin et al, 2010). This "majority" group consists of French persons born abroad and their children born abroad, which includes repatriates from the former colonial empire and their children born in France. It also includes the grandchildren of immigrants (Beauchemin et al, 2010). According to that definition, people of color born in France and of French nationality are part of the majority population.

Theoretical frames and methodologies

In order to study the grammar, mechanisms, strategies, and patterns of colorblind racism in France, this book relies on theoretical frameworks from

American sociologists Eduardo Bonilla-Silva (colorblind racism) and Joe Feagin (White racial frame). This book also refers to American sociologist Jennifer Mueller's notion of racial ignorance as an analytical tool to unpack the French context of colorblindness.

Reservations about applying American concepts and theories to a French case are understandable. Indeed, Bourdieu voiced his concerns about the importation and application of American concepts to contexts outside of the United States (1999). However, much like Jean Beaman and Amy Petts (2020), I argue that the plethora of research on race and racism across the globe shows the significance of race outside the United States and is thus relevant in other national contexts. In fact, many scholars (American and French) have demonstrated that racism persists in French society in multiple ways, including through colorblindness. Thus a cross-comparison between France and the United States is helpful to uncover how colorblind racism operates, since colorblindness is prominent in both countries. Finally, as argued by Elise Palomares (2013), despite important differences in terms of their sociohistorical trajectories, France and the United States still share some related and connected histories with regard to colonization, slavery, and labor migration. Palomares (2013) also shows that since the late 1970s, French urban sociology has developed its research notably on interethnic relations and racism in dialogue with the Chicago school tradition and other English-speaking sociology in order to apply theoretical paradigms and frameworks to the French context. It is with these considerations in mind that this book discusses and examines the case of colorblindness in contemporary France.

Contemporary American sociologists have researched the mechanisms and practices that reproduce the racial order and racial inequality. They claim that contemporary racial inequality is reproduced through "new racism" practices that are institutionalized and nonracial on the surface but maintain White supremacy. The argument here is that by appearing colorblind, such practices (which include everyday practices but also policies) hide the fact that they do discriminate against racial minorities. In turn, concealing the fact that such practices are racial and racist, and in fact constructed through a white-centered lens, makes it more challenging to prove the presence of racism, and thus sustains White supremacy while denying doing so.

White racial framing

For Feagin, systemic racism can be defined as "racial framing, discrimination, and institutional inequalities integral to White domination of people of color" (Feagin, 2010a). According to Feagin (2010a), systemic racism comprises six elements: historical and continuing patterns of unjust impoverishment and enrichment; group interests and alienating racist relations; costs and burdens of racism; vital roles of White elites; a White racial frame, allowing for the rationalization of racial oppression; and continuing resistance to racism by oppressed peoples. Indeed, on the one hand, Feagin (2010a) argues that Whites hold most positions of power (in politics, business, education, culture), and that racist views inform and shape the way Whites interact with racial minorities. As a result, Whites as a majority tend to alienate people of color through policies of discrimination, marginalization, and exclusion. In turn, these alienating racist relations make it challenging for racial minorities to achieve solidarity in order to fight systemic racism. On the other hand, Feagin (2010a) contends that the costs and burdens which are a core aspect of systemic racism disproportionately affect racial minorities, particularly Blacks. For example, limited income and wealth, limited access to educational resources, as well as police brutality and high incarceration rates, take a heavy toll on the lives of racial minorities.

Feagin (2010b: 3) defines the White racial frame as "an overarching worldview, one that encompasses important racial ideas, terms, images, emotions and interpretations." According to Feagin (2012), the White racial frame has been created to maintain and rationalize White privilege and power. In other words, White racial framing is a central support of systemic racism. White racial framing is a dominant ideology that has been perpetuated by the White elite and has provided the main vantage point from which most White people have viewed and interpreted society. However, White racial framing is much broader and deeper than just racial stereotypes and prejudices. White racial framing includes racial stereotypes and prejudices, racial narratives and interpretations, racialized imagery, racialized emotions, and a common inclination to discriminate along racial lines (Feagin, 2012). Also central to the White racial frame are "aggressively positive views of whites and their interests, folkways, and self-conceptions" (Feagin, 2012: 6).

White racial hegemony

The White racial hegemony perspective argues that systemic racism has evolved and, rather than operating in an overt way, it has become pervasive by "exercising control over cultural beliefs and ideologies, as well as the key legitimizing institutions of society through which they are expressed" (Neubeck and Cazenave, 2001: 22). White racial framing is hegemonic in its ideological form and effect so that it ensures White power and privilege. Using Dorothy Smith's (1993) terminology, we can say that White racial framing imposes its "ideological code" onto all interpretations of race and racism. As Feagin (2010b: 10) explains, "its centrality in White minds is what makes it a dominant frame."

Colorblind racism

This new system of racial practices supporting racial inequality is co-structured by a new racial ideology that Bonilla-Silva (2006) has labeled "colorblind racism."

Bonilla-Silva (2006) demonstrates that colorblind racism can be analyzed as a modern version of racism, or racism 2.0. Colorblind racism is here defined as a racial ideology, which, by minimizing the significance of race and allowing for justifications and explanations of racial inequality as a consequence of "market dynamics, naturally occurring phenomena," and supposed "cultural limitation" (Bonilla-Silva, 2006), supports and sustains White dominance and privilege in the United States.

The colorblind framework articulates powerful explanations constructed by White people that justify contemporary racial inequality and excuse them from any responsibility for the status of people of color. These explanations come from a new racial ideology called colorblind racism. This ideology, which acquired cohesion and dominance in the late 1960s, explains contemporary racial inequality as the outcome of nonracial dynamics. Specifically, Bonilla-Silva (2006) explains, colorblind ideology refers to the idea or belief that (a) racism does not exist, or is no longer a problem; (b) inequalities along racial lines are not the result of racism, but some other forms of oppression or due to personal responsibility; and (c) White people, particularly White elites and policymakers, no longer see race, and are colorblind in action and thought. Bonilla-Silva (2006) further states that colorblind ideology allows White people to rationalize minorities' contemporary status as the consequence of market dynamics, naturally occurring phenomena, and racial minorities' imputed cultural limitations. In so doing, White people can continue to make assertions that reflect and protect their racial interests but defend themselves from the accusation of being racists because the assertions themselves don't "sound" racist. Colorblindness allows White people to "express resentment toward minorities, criticize their morality, values, and work ethic, and even claim to be the victims of 'reverse racism'" (Bonilla-Silva, 2006: 4). This is what Bonilla-Silva (2006) calls "racism without racists."

In the fourth edition of *Racism without Racists* (2014), Bonilla-Silva writes:

> Much as Jim Crow racism served as the glue for defending a brutal and overt system of racial oppression in the pre-civil rights era, colorblind racism serves today as the ideological armor for a covert and institutionalized system in the post-civil rights era. And the beauty of this new ideology is that it aids in the maintenance of white privilege without fanfare, without naming those who it subjects and those who it rewards. (2014: 3–4)

While the ideas of "White racial frame" and "colorblind racism" have been developed by American scholars in reference to American society, the concept of "frame" behind each theory offers a relevant basis for an analysis of the French context. As this book will demonstrate, the frames used by the French government serve as dominant "paths for interpreting information" (Bonilla-Silva, 2006: 26). And while scholars have used the idea of colorblindness to study patterns of discrimination in France (Stovall, 1993), to analyze the French model of integration (Bleich, 2001), or to explain the absence of ethnic statistics in the French census (Sabbagh and Peer, 2008), no other French studies have used Bonilla-Silva's colorblind racism framework in a comprehensive analysis of the French case of colorblind racism.

The theory of racial ignorance

For J. Mueller (2017), in addition to focusing on the structural elements of colorblindness, we also need to examine the mechanisms of what she calls "White ignorance," defined as a "process of knowing designed to produce not knowing surrounding White privilege and structural White supremacy." In this context, ignorance is more than a vacuum or a gap in knowledge. It is a "social product in its own right" that influences "human cognition, emotion, action, social relations, and culture" (Smithson, 2008: 209).

Mueller (2017) frames ignorance as an epistemological accomplishment that relies on a paradox in that for hegemonic ideologies to maintain their hegemony, they must hide their dominance and remain ignored. Indeed, as argued by Mueller (2017), the structure of White supremacy calls for colorblindness, or not seeing race. And colorblindness is precisely about "sustaining an ignorance useful for cloaking and reproducing structural mechanics of white supremacy." In some ways, this can be connected to Simon's notion of the "choice of ignorance" (2008) with regard to the removal of any reference to race or ethnicity from all policies, laws, and census data. Mueller (2017) is only suggesting that scholars should not underestimate "whites' psychic commitment to accomplishing racial ignorance." In fact, Mueller says that "ignorance is the foundation of white thinking" (2020: 143).

Social construction

Throughout the book, I intend to unpack representations, discourses, symbols, typologies, processes, and categories that tell us something about the realities as they are experienced but also constructed by individuals and institutions. This is not to say that there aren't objective social facts taking place in the world. And this book certainly takes into account the reality of the social world. However, through the lens of social constructivism, we must acknowledge and examine how meanings are ascribed and contested by different social actors and how individuals receive these meanings. We must also recognize and analyze how these meanings are rendered through relational social processes and what the contentions around these social processes signify and imply.

Methodologies

Capturing the complexity of such phenomena demands a diversity of methods. My methodological approach thus includes quantitative and qualitative analysis, particularly examining official statistics, political speeches, historical accounts, media reports, and academic discourses. The objective is to unpack and discuss the different levels of discourses produced by places and institutions that construct the dominant narratives about race in France, so that we better understand the mechanisms of reproduction behind colorblind racism in French society.

Conclusion

Through its examination of French history, this chapter has noted that – contrary to what French political pundits might say – race is not an idea imported from the United States, or a dangerous idea originating in fascist regimes during the Second World War, and there isn't a supposed trend about the "black question" in France (Tobner, 2007) in the sense that it is not part of a latest popular and passing item in the news coming from external forces. The use of the notion of race in French dates back to the 1500s, as part of the colonial project of the French state. In fact, as seen in this chapter, it is in the context of the construction of a French colonial empire, and the emergence of racist ideologies justifying the colonial enterprise, that the word race first appeared in France. The numerous debates among French demographers over the use of racial categories in data collection show the problematic nature of the notion of race in French society and of thinking about, and let alone finding common grounds to address, the issues of racism and discrimination in France.

In other words, in contemporary France we are witnessing a denegation, a choice of ignorance, that race exists and that it is a central structuring component of French social and political life. This choice of colorblindness leads to the persistence of colorblind racism, which significantly impacts French racial minorities, as discussed in the subsequent chapters.

3

The French Model of Integration and Colorblind Racism

In response to the death of George Floyd, an African American man murdered by the police on May 25, 2020, and remembering the death of Adama Traoré, a Malian French man who died in custody after being apprehended by the police on July 19, 2016, French President Macron declared during a Minister's Council that racism and discrimination were a "plague that is a betrayal to the republican universalism" and a "disease that touches all of society." He also asked his ministers to be "uncompromising on the topic" and to "reinforce action" against racism (*Le Monde*, June 10, 2020).

This statement may appear somewhat puzzling, since France presents itself as a colorblind society at the macro level. For example, as said earlier, France has eliminated the word race from its Constitution, and as Chapter 3 explains at length, France also forbids the collection of ethnic statistics for the census. Therefore, we might expect a colorblind society to be immune to racism and discrimination since it excludes race from its institutional vocabulary and policies. But President Macron's statement clearly indicates that racism is in fact very much present in French society.

We need to look at the contradictions between the republican ideal of colorblind equality, which supports and sustains French integration policies, and the actual discrimination as perceived and experienced by French racial minorities in France, as well as their stigmatization as members of racial minority groups. It is important to note that because of the lack of official ethno-racial categorizations, it has been challenging for French social scientists to examine racial discrimination and racism patterns among French racial minorities. In fact, as expressed in the introduction of this book, immigrants and French racial minorities are often used and understood by the media and the larger public as largely synonymous categories when addressing race, racism, and racial groups at the macro and micro levels. This conflation renders the study of discrimination patterns among French racial minorities rather confusing. This confusion also participates in the reproduction of colorblind racism, as the lack of appropriate data collection and measurement prevents social scientists from examining the structuring effect that these discriminatory practices produce and perpetuate.

This chapter will first provide a description of France's contemporary demography, with a particular focus on French nationals rather than immigrants. The chapter will also review the current structures in place, including legal measures against discrimination in France. Finally, it will review current research by social scientists examining patterns of racial discrimination and segregation within French society today, particularly as this affects employment, housing, education, health, and policing against French racial minorities.

Clarification and caveat

However, first, as a point of clarification, this book focuses specifically on issues of race, racism, and racial inequality as they pertain to French nationals, since many social science studies already exist that examine racism and discrimination as experienced by immigrants in France. That notwithstanding, one of the major challenges in studying race in France is that notions of racial identity or ethnicity are often conflated with immigrant status rather than being applied to all French citizens. As a consequence, it initially appears that French citizens, both the majority population and minorities, have no race and therefore that racism cannot exist as French society is raceless and/or colorblind. But this couldn't be any further from the socioeconomic and political reality that individuals experience on a daily basis, and that French social scientists have observed using alternative methods to account for the relevance of race and the significance of racism, with and despite the prevalence of colorblindness in French society. Second, we must acknowledge that the divide between French nationals and immigrants in how we examine colorblind racism can be problematic as well. Indeed, the term immigrant in France is often used by politicians and the media as a proxy for race, and assumptions of immigrant status are based on the color of the skin, where nonWhite individuals are viewed as immigrants but White individuals are not. The same is true for assumptions made about French nationals, where White persons are presumed to be French nationals but nonWhite persons are not. Thus we must recognize that such a divide is already a social construction inherent to French society, despite the French model's pretension of not seeing race.

It is from this paradoxical point that the book will be articulated and attempt to untangle the different discourses and realities.

Contemporary demography of France

For social scientists in France, capturing racial discrimination and segregation patterns of French people of color is a challenging task, as data on race or ethnicity are not collected in the French census. Indeed, while completing the French census has been mandatory since 1946, the census does not allow for the collection of racial or ethnic data. Questions in the French census about a person's origins only deal with place of birth and national identity, which only allows a distinction to be made between French nationals, immigrants, and foreigners. Some surveys outside of the official census also collect data on the descendants of immigrants, but as noted by Simon (2012, Migration Policy Institute), these are limited and don't always allow for precise interpretation and analysis.

For the purpose of this book, I will use the following definitions, also used by demographer Patrick Simon and the L'Institut National d'Etudes Démographiques (INED, or French Institute for Demographic Studies) (also included in the Glossary).

- Immigrants: persons born abroad with a foreign nationality at birth. This definition excludes French citizens born abroad (children of expatriates, former colonizers). The Institut National de la Statistique et des Etudes Economiques (INSEE, or National Institute of Statistics and Economic Studies) specifies that the immigrant population includes individuals who may have acquired French nationality since their arrival. Nonetheless, they are still counted as immigrants.
- Descendants of immigrants: persons born and residing in metropolitan France with a least one immigrant parent.
- Départements d'Outre Mer (DOM, or Overseas Departments) native-born: persons born in one of the French overseas departments.
- Descendants of DOM native-born: persons born in metropolitan France with at least one parent born in a DOM.
- Mainstream population: persons who are not immigrants or descendants of one or more immigrants or who are not DOM native-born or descendants of one or more DOM native-born. Most of the mainstream population is born in metropolitan France with two parents born in metropolitan France, but the group also includes French citizens born abroad (repatriates from the former French colonies or children of expatriates).
- Foreigners: persons without French citizenship.

Additionally, a study by Simon in 2012 on French national identity used a survey where one of the categories is "persons born in mainland France without immigrant background, from two generations."

Finally, an INED study by Beauchemain et al (2010) on the perception of discrimination experienced by individuals in France uses the following categories:

- Immigrant: person born foreign in a foreign country and residing in France. They may have French nationality if they acquired it after migrating, or they may have kept their foreign nationality.
- Minorities: generic designation that includes immigrants, persons born in the departments of Overseas France, and the persons who are their sons and daughters.
- Majority population: all the French nationals who are not immigrants, or sons and daughters of immigrants or persons born in Overseas France. This group comprises French nationals born abroad and their children, which includes repatriates from the former colonial empire and their children born in metropolitan France. It also includes the grandchildren of immigrants.

According to the 2020 French census estimates (INSEE, 2021a), France counts 67.3 million inhabitants. Table 3.1 provides a breakdown of the population counted in the census as residing in France in 2020.

Another INSEE study (2021b) specifically examining the immigrant and foreign population in France operates the following divisions. On the one hand, this INSEE study (2021b) claims that there are 6.8 million immigrants in France or 10.2 percent of the total population in France (see Table 3.2).

On the other hand, the same INSEE study (2021b) evaluates at 5.1 million the number of foreigners in France or 7.6 percent of the total population (see Table 3.3).

And then finally, yet another INSEE study (2020) includes the notion of "descendants of immigrants" (person born and residing in France who

Table 3.1: Population residing in France, 2020

Nationality/place of birth	Millions	Percentage
French nationals born in France	58,001	86.2
Immigrants born abroad, naturalized French	2,462	3.7
Immigrants born abroad, foreign nationals	4,369	6.5
Foreigners born in France	0.768	1.1
French nationals born abroad	1,687	2.5
TOTAL POPULATION IN FRANCE	**67,287**	**100**

Source: INSEE, Décomposition de la population vivant en France en 2020 (2021a): https://www.insee.fr/fr/statistiques/2865118

Table 3.2: Immigrant and foreign population in France, 2021

Status	Millions	Percentage
Immigrants, naturalized French	2.5	36
Immigrants, foreign nationals	4.5	64
TOTAL IMMIGRANT POPULATION	**7.00**	**100**

Source: INSEE, Décomposition de la population vivant en France en 2020 (2021a): https://www.insee.fr/fr/statistiques/3633212

Table 3.3: Foreign nationals and foreigners born in France, 2021

Status	Millions	Percentage
Immigrants, foreign nationals	4.5	84
Foreigners born in France	0.8	16
TOTAL FOREIGN POPULATION	**5.2**	**100**

Source: INSEE, Décomposition de la population vivant en France en 2020 (2021a): https://www.insee.fr/fr/statistiques/3633212

Table 3.4: Geographical origins of immigrants in France, 2020

3.2 million or 47.5% come from Africa
2.1 million or 32.2% come from Europe
979,000 or 14.4% come from Asia
394,000 or 5.8% come from the Americas/Oceania

Source: INSEE, Décomposition de la population vivant en France en 2020 (2021a): https://www.insee.fr/fr/statistiques/3633212

has at least one immigrant parent, see Glossary): according to this study, France counted 7.6 million descendants of immigrants (or 11.5 percent of the total French population) in 2019, with half of the descendants having two immigrant parents.

In summary, following the INSEE data, we can deduce that the French population comprises:

- 60 million French nationals or members of the mainstream population (with no immigrant ascendants);
- 2.5 million immigrants who are naturalized French;
- 7.6 million descendants of immigrants; and
- 5.1 million foreigners.

Table 3.4 sets out the geographical origins of the 10.2 percent of immigrants residing in France.

Table 3.5: Geographical origins of descendants of immigrants in France, 2020

3.4 million or 45.4% originate from Africa
3.1 million or 40.9% originate from Europe
745 thousand or 9.7% originate from Asia
300 thousand or 3.9% originate from the Americas/Oceania

Source: INSEE, Décomposition de la population vivant en France en 2020 (2021a): https://www.insee.fr/fr/statistiques/3633212

And Table 3.5 outlines the geographical origins of the 11.5 percent of descendants of immigrants residing in France.

Without any official data on ethnicity or race, and only using the numbers cited above from the French census, it is immediately apparent that accounting for ethnic groups among French citizens, and not just immigrants, is confusing, challenging, and an exercise in approximation. Moreover, attempting to identify French racial minorities is rendered complicated because it initially seems as if the only populations with any identified ethnicity or ethnic ascendance are immigrants, descendants of immigrants, or the foreign population. Consequently, the majority or mainstream population – defined as not immigrants and not descendants of immigrants – is presumed to have no ethnicity. In other words, using this official data, the idea of ethnic identity, let alone racial identity, seems to be reserved for immigrant and foreign population groups. In that sense, it looks as if the state is in fact colorblind.

It follows that the data provided by the French census does not permit for a clear or precise examination of French racial minorities in terms of categories. In such a context, it is equally challenging for social scientists to reflect France's racial diversity and report and analyze the patterns of racial discrimination minorities face.

Current French laws on discrimination and diversity

French legal scholar Danièle Lochak (1987: 778) gives the following legal definition of discrimination as "the illegitimate distinction or difference in treatment: illegitimate because arbitrary, and forbidden because illegitimate."

French demographer Simon (with INED) similarly defines discrimination as "unfavorable treatment based on an illegitimate and possibly illegal criteria." Simon (2014) also specifies that discrimination "amounts to a penalty for characteristics that should not be taken into account in hiring or access to goods," among which are sex, ethnic or racial origin, nationality, religion, sexual orientation, disability, and health issues.

The Defender of Rights (Défenseur des Droits)– an independent administrative authority (nominated by the French President) that aims to defend the rights of French citizens in front of administrations (like an ombudsman), as well as to promote children's rights and fight against discrimination and other matters – gives the legal definition of discrimination as an "unfavorable treatment that must include two cumulative conditions: it must be based on a criteria as defined by the law AND fall within a situation aimed by the law" (Défenseur des Droits, nd, original emphasis). The law now recognizes more than 25 criteria of discrimination: for example, national origin, sex, age, disability, opinions, pregnancy, health, genetic characteristics, sexual orientation, gender identity, and the "true or supposed belonging or nonbelonging to an ethnic group, a nation or an alleged race." These criteria actually emanate from international and European legislation, while other criteria only come from within the French jurisdiction (for example, last name, physical appearance, family situation, residential address, capacity to express oneself in a language other than French). Among other things, the situations for which discrimination is considered include access to work, career, salary, social benefits, access to housing, access to banking, access to public education and healthcare, and access to places welcoming public audiences (private and public institutions).

The Observatoire des Inégalités (Inequality Observatory), another independent organization, founded in 2003, whose scientific committee is composed of sociologists (partly in reaction to the presence of far-right leader Jean-Marie Le Pen in the second round of French presidential elections), seeks to examine and analyze inequality patterns through data collection in France and Europe. The organization defines discrimination as a "difference in treatment forbidden by law" (Observatoire des Inégalités, 2022: 2) and includes several criteria (among which are sex, age, origin, health status, sexual orientation, political opinions, and so on). It also specifies that discrimination is contrary to the most fundamental principle of equality, the equality of citizens' rights that is at the center of the French Constitution and French democracy.

Since the 1970s, several antiracism measures and policies have been implemented in France, largely under the impulse of international legal norms (Bereni and Chappe, 2011). Notably, the 1972 Pleven Law (72-546) against racism bans discrimination and racist acts in private and public life and punishes perpetrators in criminal courts with heavy fines and prison sentences. According to Laure Bereni and Vincent-Arnaude Chappe (2011), the 1972 law was the first piece of legislation to introduce into the French Penal Code the principle of nondiscrimination based on "membership of an ethnic group, a nation, a race or a specific religion."

Another significant law is the 1990 Gayssot Law or Gayssot Act (90-615), which reinforces the penalties against racist acts and adds to the list of crimes classified as racist. In particular, the Gayssot Act is intended to punish all racist, anti-Semitic, or xenophobic acts. It is the first "memorial law" in that it explicitly refers to events that are part of French national history, and specifically anti-Semitism during the Second World War. Indeed, the law punishes anyone contesting or denying the existence of crimes against humanity as defined by the Nuremberg International Military Tribunal.

Article 1 of the 2008 Law (2008-496) regarding dispositions in the fight against discrimination declares that direct discrimination can be defined as

a situation in which, based on their membership or non-membership, true or presupposed, of an ethnic group or a race, based on their religion, their convictions, their age, their handicap, their sexual orientation or their sex, a person is treated less favorably than another is, was, or will be, in a comparable situation.

Article 1 of the 2008 law on discrimination also defines indirect discrimination as

a disposition, criteria or practice that is neutral in appearance, but susceptible of leading to a particular disadvantage for some individuals compared with other individuals, unless this disposition, criteria, or practice is objectively justified by a legitimate goal, and that the means to realize that goal are necessary and appropriate.

Legal measures concerning the relations between employers and employees include Article L1132-1 of the Labor Code (Code du Travail), which makes discrimination illegal when hiring workers. In its 2020 modification, Article 15 of the Labor Code states that

no individual can be excluded from a hiring process or nomination or access to an internship or to a company training, no employee can be sanctioned, fired, or be the object of a discriminatory measure, direct or indirect ... because of their origin, their sex, their morals, their sexual orientation, their gender identity, their age, their family situation, their pregnancy, ..., their true or presumed membership or non-membership to an ethnicity, a nation, or a supposed race ..., their religious convictions, their physical appearance, their family name, their place of residence, ... their capacity to express themselves in a language other than French.

Therefore, for treatment to be considered as discrimination, a link must be established to the just-mentioned criteria (Masclet, 2017).

Furthermore, in 1999, at the government's initiative, several independent organizations were created to examine, analyze, explain, and combat discrimination based on (but not limited to) race and ethnicity: for example, the Groupe d'Etude et de Lutte contre les Discriminations (GELD, or Group of Study and Fight against Discriminations), Departmental Commission for Access to Citizenship (CODAC, Commission Départementale d'Accès à la Citoyenneté), and Funds for Action and Support of Integration and Fight against Discriminations (FASILD, or Fond d'Aide et de Soutien pour l'Intégration et la Lutte contre les Discriminations) are entities bringing together politicians, scholars, and members of civil society to discuss issues related to racism and discrimination. In 2000, the government established a free hotline to collect grievances from individuals who were victims of racial discrimination and who might want to engage in lawsuits. Following that path, after a 2001 law was passed, employers accused of racial discrimination had the burden of proof of their innocence, whereas it had previously been the reverse. Finally, a law of December 30, 2004 proclaimed that everyone had "the right to equal treatment, regardless of his/her national origin, his/her membership, real or presupposed, in an ethnic group or a race." And it is this same law that also ratified the creation of the French Equal Opportunities and Anti-Discrimination Commission, Haute autorité de lutte contre les discriminations et pour l'égalité (HALDE, or French Equal Opportunities and Anti-Discrimination Commission). The case of HALDE actually raises some interesting contradictions. As an independent administrative institution, HALDE's mission was to address and investigate all cases of direct or indirect discrimination and promote equal rights on all French territories. The 18 criteria of discrimination considered illegal were origin, sex, family status, pregnancy status, physical appearance, last name, health status, disability, genetic characteristics, morals, sexual orientation, age, political opinions, and workers' union activities, as well as membership, real or assumed, of a particular ethnic group, nation, race, or religion. However, despite the underlying acknowledgment of the existence of race and ethnicity as possible criteria of discrimination, HALDE fiercely opposed the inclusion of ethnic and racial data in census statistics and other data-gathering processes. HALDE was dismantled in 2011 when its main activity was incorporated under the authority of the Defender of Rights, the overall mission of which is to ensure "respect for the rights and freedoms" of French citizens, as per Article 71-1 of the French Constitution. Thus, unlike HALDE, the Defender of Rights does not have a specific focus on racial discrimination.

Finally, a new online platform called "antidiscriminations" created by the Defender of Rights provides a space for individuals to report discrimination (in employment, housing, and so on), violence (racist, sexist, anti-Semitic, homophobic, and so forth), or even hate speech (Défenseur des Droits, nd).

Apart from antidiscrimination policies, and as part of policies addressing inequalities, France has used positive discrimination, which is defined by the Observatoire des Inégalités (2005) as a set of measures and policies targeting specific groups in society lacking equal access to public services in order to rectify these inequalities. The Observatoire des Inégalités (2005) adds that it is essentially a "refocusing of the welfare state" with three objectives: adjusting conditions between unequal groups, combating discrimination in all areas of society (but particularly employment), and promoting diversity. For Baptiste Villenave (2006), positive discrimination can be defined as a set of measures and practices to eliminate past or current inequalities to which certain groups are subjected by temporarily granting some specific preferential treatments and quotas, for example with regard to job recruitment. Villenave (2006) further states that the goal of positive discrimination is to correct, through specific programs such as quotas, the disadvantages certain groups have accumulated over generations, because "the mechanisms of social reproduction" mean that some groups are overrepresented in higher education or in certain jobs. In that regard, positive discrimination has been compared with the affirmative action policies developed in the United States in the 1960s.

However, there is currently only one specific law that qualifies as positive discrimination, the February 11, 2005 law (or law no. 2005–102 for "the equality of rights and chances, the participation and citizenship of disabled persons"). This law applies to the employment of disabled individuals. It was initially put in place in 1987 and applied to the private sector, with the 2005 law expanding it to public administrations and other public institutions. It requires that all employers offer 6 percent of their total jobs to disabled individuals. Should companies or administrations not meet this quota, financial sanctions will be applied. This was followed by a law passed on January 27, 2011 law (or law no. 2011-103 "relative to the balanced representation between women and men on board of directors and relative to the professional equality"), which aims to promote the presence of women in board rooms for companies of more than 500 employees and earning more than 50 million euros (sometimes requiring quotas to be met). But outside of these groups, there are no provisions in these laws with specific references to race or racial minority groups. In fact, since the mid-1990s, the classical forms of state intervention toward equality, such as quotas and subsidies, have been considered obsolete, as the job market for employees has expanded to the European Union, where work policies are not homogenized. Instead, as Gwénaële Calvès (2004) explains, various policies, practices, and techniques are applied on a case-by-case basis in terms of positive discrimination targeting racial minorities. For example, starting in 2001, the elite political science school in Paris (Institut d'études politiques [IEP]) started a program of positive discrimination by signing an agreement, the Convention éducation prioritaire (CEP, or Convention of Priority Education). This special agreement opened the admission process of the IEP to high school students from disenfranchised zones (Zone éducation prioritaire): rather than having to take a competitive admission exam as is usually required for such a school, high school students from disenfranchised zones are recruited based on their application file and an interview. The elite school of business and economic sciences (Ecole supérieure des sciences économiques et commerciales) launched a similar program. And since 2005, the prestigious elite Parisian high school Lycée Henri IV has set aside preparatory classes (preparing for the grandes ecoles, French elite higher education institutions with competitive admission) specifically for scholarship students (presumably from lower socioeconomic backgrounds).

In 2006, Nicolas Sarkozy, the candidate for the right wing Union pour un Mouvement Populaire party (UMP, Union for a Popular Movement) for the 2007 presidential elections, declared that

> administrations are required by law to hire 6% of their collaborators with a disability. What is it if not a quota? I'd like someone to tell me why it would be normal to apply positive discrimination for women or disabled people, and why it wouldn't be normal for our compatriots of color? (*Le Parisien*, October 20, 2006)

However, in January 2007 he declared that he was opposed to any form of positive discrimination based on skin color, claiming that he didn't want a form of "communitarianism that reduces man to a sole visible identity" (UMP Congress, January 14, 2007).

In terms of addressing inequalities and disparities in employment and education, France considers it more efficient to focus on geography and the place of residence (disenfranchised neighborhoods) than on racial or ethnic characteristics. The focus is therefore placed on socioeconomic background rather than explicitly addressing racial inequalities, with the implicit assumption that social class plays a more significant role in discrimination.

However, the term positive discrimination is itself problematic because it implies that discrimination can be beneficial to society, when most individuals and groups experience negative consequences from discrimination. It also implies that measures and policies that help address structural and systemic racism are still a form of discrimination that benefits some but is to the detriment of others. Second, as a set of political measures and laws intending to counter and correct discrimination due to socioeconomic and residential patterns, the very idea of positive discrimination seems to contradict the way France presents itself as colorblind, where race or ethnicity have no place in society and thus no impact on a person's chances of success. However, using Bonilla-Silva's approach (2006), we can analyze the setup of positive discrimination policies in France as colorblind racism: indeed, using Bonilla-Silva's concept of the minimization frame, we can interpret the French government's position as trying to minimize the significance of race and racism by instead focusing its efforts on social class. A colorblind ideology will indeed defend the idea that inequalities affecting racial minorities are not the result of racism but rather some other form of oppression, such as social class, as Stephen Ostertag and William Armaline demonstrate (2011). Third, as argued by Villenave (2006), the question of positive discrimination policies is presented and dealt with by the French state as a problem solely regarding the immigrant population in France: in fact, Villenave (2006) claims, the main goal of such measures seems to be not only to rectify inequalities toward marginalized populations but also to promote the integration of immigrants. In other words, positive discrimination is discussed as a means of allowing immigrants to better integrate into French society: it is thus framed in terms of an immigration problem rather than the state's failure to provide equal access to resources and socioeconomic justice to French racial minorities. It also allows the state to avoid talking about race. Finally, according to Villenave (2006), the question of positive discrimination is connected to this idea of representation and diversity in French society. That is, by establishing quotas, Villenave (2006) argues, the French state is attempting to get closer to the ideal of a "mirrored representation," or for all groups of people living in France to be represented in schools, at work, and within public institutions, hence reflecting the diversity of France's population. However, as Calvès (2005) argues, the idea that administrations should be "reflecting the diversity of the French population" is a foreign and new notion. Indeed, the idea that public administration should be representative of the population is not part of French administrative culture, Calvès (2005) claims, but is an American concept that was only adopted in the 1980s. Before that time, Calvès (2005) claims, the administrative ideology in France was based on the idea that the role of the public service administration was to serve the interests of the nation, not the needs of specific groups of the population. In the same spirit, for example, the elite Ecole Nationale d'Administration (ENA, National School of Administration, founded in 1945 by French President Charles de Gaulle) isn't expected to reflect the demographics of the French population but to be the "mirror of the State" (Gaillard, 1995). And so, the idea of promoting racial diversity is first and foremost presented and defended as a way to support policies designed to integrate immigrants into French society rather than addressing the issue of racial discrimination and representation.

As explained by Bleich (2000), French antiracist or antidiscrimination policies and institutions correspond to and are influenced by the wish to seek out colorblind, race-neutral principles and therefore to avoid treating race as real and central to French society. For example, the 1972 law does not contain any race-conscious elements but instead focuses on criminal penalties for racist actions. Bleich claims that these colorblind policies may in fact "exemplify an antiracism without races" (2000: 50). He argues that French law was designed to punish racist acts rather than foster racial equality. Indeed, the focus of French antiracist laws is on the fight against hate speech to the detriment of direct and effective measures against job or housing discrimination and institutional racism.

Discrimination patterns in contemporary France

Demographic and sociological studies published by French social scientists use data based on the kinds of census surveys and definitions stated in the previous section because no other kinds of definitions are available that would include racial categories.

Other analyses include studies measuring respondents' perceived experience of discrimination (Beauchemin et al, 2010; Pan Ké Shon and Scodellaro, 2011; Brinbaum et al, 2012; Simon, 2012).

As noted by Palomares (2013), the categories of populations by nationality of ancestry (whether regional or continental) created and used by the French census become euphemisms in lieu of race and racialized groups, which is problematic because it focuses on and groups immigrants and descendants of immigrants at the same level. Additionally, this type of categorization, which focuses solely on nationality and immigration status, implies that there are no people of color among the "mainstream" population. Therefore, all subsequent data in support of this book's analysis shows information according to the French census's classifications, which also demonstrate the limitations that social scientists face when examining discrimination patterns in France.

Discrimination based on origin, which is the only form of discrimination really measured in France, can be obtained in the following three ways: see Masclet, 2017.

Public surveys (INSEE)

Article 8-I of the 1978 Informatique et Libertés Law stipulates that it is forbidden to collect data on personal characteristics that would show "directly or indirectly" someone's "ethnic or racial origins," among other things. Not respecting this law can incur a penalty of up to 300,000 euros according to Article 226-19 of the Penal Code. However, there are some exceptions to this law – for example, if individuals give written consent to be asked about their origins or skin color. Thus, using such individual consent, research institutes such as INSEE and other public research institutes are able to collect ethnic statistics after their research proposal has been approved by the Commission Nationale informatique et Libertés (CNIL, or National Commission on Informatics and Liberty) and the Conseil national de l'information statistique (CNIS, National Council of Statistic Information). These two committees have the authority to examine research proposals case by case, according to the objectives of the research, the consent of the people interviewed, and the anonymity of the data.

Therefore, while the French census does not include racial categories, but only the national origin of citizens, social science research can incorporate the notion of racial membership into questionnaires and data.

For example, the Trajectoire et origine (TeO, or "Trajectory and origin") survey carried out by INSEE and INED in 2008–9 on a population sample of 21,000 people in France used the birthplace and nationality of individuals and their parents in order to study social integration and discrimination (Simon and Safi, 2013). The survey examined the social conditions and status of immigrants, the mainstream population, and respondents' self-reported experience of discrimination with regard to access to work, housing, education, and healthcare.

According to French demographer François Héran (Masclet, 2017), these statistics do not necessarily represent accurately the notion of discrimination, and it might be preferrable to refer to the idea of ethnic penalty for some of the disenfranchised populations in France. Indeed, according to Héran (Masclet, 2017), discrimination is too generic a term in that it does not specifically focus on the ethnicity of the populations.

Testing

Testing is another way in which French scholars study inequalities linked to the origin of an individual. It is an experimental method recreating a discriminatory situation, for example in the job market: the point is to test job applications sent to employers, where applications are identical with the exception of one criterion for which the candidate is likely to face discrimination, such as skin color, name, or address, as most French CVs include a photo of the candidate as well as a personal address. Therefore, the goal is to catch discrimination as it happens in empirical life. And in this case, the focus is on the person or institution discriminating against others. This way of shifting the question eliminates any doubt about the existence of inequality in treatment, since discrimination is established as soon as the person committing the discrimination carries out their judgment based on one controlled criterion. Results have shown that discrimination based on skin color, patronyms, or address is indeed widespread in all professional sectors and at all educational levels and positions.

However, testing only indicates the presence of discrimination at a specific moment in time during the experiment and for a specific field and does not show the state of racial discrimination in general for the entire field. Furthermore, testing is not able to account for inequalities in salaries, promotions, and other related career patterns throughout an individual's life. Finally, human resources offices have found a way to circumvent any accusation of discrimination by systematically selecting one minority candidate's CV whom they will end up not hiring but that will skew the numbers in terms of representation and data.

Studies based on first and last names

In 2001, French sociologist Georges Félouzis carried out a survey to analyze ethnic segregation in middle school in the region of Bordeaux in France, simply using students' first names. The rationale was that in order to examine possible dysfunctions and penalties in the educational system, national origin was not a sufficient criterion because many students had acquired French nationality. Thus, Félouzis constructed three "ethnic origin" categories of students based on deduction from their first names: "allochtons" (or foreign-born), that is, students whose names are most typically given in the Maghreb, sub-Saharan Africa, and Turkey; "other allochtons," that is, students whose names are most typically given in Southern Europe, Southeast Asia, and Eastern Europe; and finally, "autochtons" (or native-born), that is, students whose names are typically given in France. The heterogeneity of these categories was connected to the goal of the survey, namely measuring the level of discrimination and prejudice felt and experienced by individuals. The findings were that foreign-born students felt and experienced significant levels of discrimination and prejudice, while native-born students felt and experienced almost no discrimination or prejudice. The method was considered so successful at revealing the experience of discrimination that it was subsequently used to analyze judicial decisions, electoral dynamics, and discriminatory practices in companies (Masclet, 2017: 48).

However, this method is problematic for a number of reasons. First, the decision to focus on first names is not reliable, as studies have shown that descendants of immigrants have strategized to give traditional French-sounding names to their children, instead of traditional names found in their country (this is especially true for Maghrebi first names). The approach has also been heavily criticized by other French sociologists (Hervé Le Bras, Alain Blum) for its lack of scientific rigor.

In all of these cases, the criteria used serve as proxies for race or ethnicity and may prove useful to identify some level of penalty or disadvantage. However, the use of such criteria in social sciences and governmental agencies raises at least three issues: (1) qualifying such penalties as racial discrimination depends on the subjective appreciation of the authors of the study rather than on objective criteria; (2) it establishes a conflation between ethnicity and immigrants as well as their descendants but does not clearly include French citizens, as if to imply that ethnicity only concerns immigrant populations, and not all French citizens, and by extension, neither studying discrimination among them; (3) it reinforces the denial of the significance of race as a social category and central force of structured inequality in French society. In fact, by using only last names and first names as a proxy for race or ethnicity, it is assumed that ethnicity only concerns and includes immigrants with foreign-sounding last names, and not all French citizens that may not have foreign-sounding last names. This last name criteria also assumes, therefore, that studying discrimination only applies to people with foreign-sounding last names, as if people who don't have a foreign-sounding last name didn't have an ethnicity, and couldn't experience discrimination.

Nonetheless, these methods and studies, as currently used by French scholars, have demonstrated the existence of penalties against immigrants and their descendants from the Maghreb, sub-Saharan Africa, and Turkey. Such findings confirm that a person's national origin constitutes a disadvantage on the job market (Simon and Safi, 2013).

Along with legislation against racism and discrimination, a number of affirmative action policies started to be implemented in France in the 1980s. The French terminology corresponding to the American notion is "positive discrimination" and designates a set of diverse measures applied to fight against socioeconomic inequalities and encourage greater diversity in education and different sectors of the economy. However, as Bleich (2011) notes, it is only recently that the ethnic dimensions have been debated with regard to such measures. For example, in 2001, the Institut d'Etudes Politiques (or "Sciences Po" political science school) created some special recruitment policies with the objective of enrolling more ethnic minorities to its student population. Other elite schools followed the trend, starting in 2005 (Masclet, 2017). That being said, Bleich (2011) explains that schools like Sciences Po did not in fact explicitly include racial criteria in their student enrollment methods; rather, Sciences Po's initiative is only geographically based, focusing on underserved and disenfranchised areas. The idea behind it is to remain race-neutral, which is why Calvès (2000) calls French positive discrimination strictly colorblind. Socioeconomic criteria are the sole focus of positive discrimination measures, with the implication that individuals from lower socioeconomic backgrounds also reside in disenfranchised and/ or lower-income communities and that some of these residents may also be ethnic minorities. But this last consideration is viewed as an incidental correlation that policies should not focus on.

Employment discrimination

Numerous studies (Weil, 2005; Castel, 2007; Hargreaves, 2007) have shown that French people of color experience economic, residential, and political marginalization and exclusion on the basis of their perceived or presumed race based on their skin color.

More specifically, several studies (Weil, 2005; Castel, 2007; Hargreaves, 2007; Fassin and Fassin, 2009; Beauchemin et al, 2010; Athari et al, 2019) have shown the existence of discrimination in the job market due to national origin in recruitment, promotion, and pay. Furthermore, Anthony Edo and Nicolas Jacquemet (2013) claim that numerous empirical fieldwork studies have long shown the existence of discriminatory behavior from employers toward "visible minorities," as racial minorities are often called in France (Riach and Rich, 2002; Bertrand and Mullainathan, 2005; Oreopoulos, 2011; Lang and Lehmann, 2012).

A 1998 report by the Haut Conseil à l'Intégration (HCI, High Council for Integration) explicitly recognizes that most forms of discrimination affect "French people of color, notably from overseas French territories or of non-European foreign origin." Fassin (2002) explains that this is a recognition that the basis for those inequalities is racial in nature and therefore that races are socially relevant and significant.

In 2006, the Observatory of Discriminations (Observatoire des Discriminations) published the results of a survey showing that the CV of a job candidate with a foreign-sounding last name but without a photo was three times less likely to receive an answer than a candidate with a White, French-sounding name (although the euphemism often used instead of the racial category "White French" is "of French stock").

Robert Castel (2007) notes that French citizens of extra-European origins had higher unemployment rates than White French and in some instances higher than foreigners: for example, Castel (2007) compared unemployment numbers in major French cities (see Table 3.6).

Castel (2007) explains that through the testing method, for job candidates or housing applications, social scientists have been able to demonstrate the existence of discrimination based on the presumed names, national origin, residence, or photos of the tested individuals. He notes that individuals with presumed characteristics (through either their names or photo or residence) of someone of North African or sub-Saharan African origins are five times less likely to obtain a positive response on their job or housing application than an individual with characteristics presumed to be of a White person. Similarly, Alec Hargreaves (2007: 43) also shows that "postcolonial minorities" are socioeconomically disadvantaged with high unemployment levels.

A 2010 study published in the INED demography journal *Populations et Sociétés* (Beauchemin et al, 2010) notes that a quarter of the immigrants and children of immigrants surveyed declared having experienced discrimination ("sexist, racist, homophobic, linked to age, to religion, or health"). More specifically, in order of importance, they cite discrimination based on origin or nationality (37 percent), and then skin color (20 percent).

Table 3.6: Unemployment rates in France by nationality and race, 1999

Nationality/race	Lyon	Marseille	Paris	Lille
White French	19%	33%	17%	29%
French with extra-European origins	37%	58%	29%	42%
Foreigners	34%	51%	28%	48%

Source: Castel (2007)

Similarly, Duguet et al (2010) have observed a discrimination rate of 35 percent toward job candidates of Maghrebi origins meaning that 35 percent of job candidates of Maghrebi origins have experienced discrimination during the hiring process. In 2013, Edo and Jacquemet also published a study explaining how, all things being equal (qualifications, years of experience, education level), employers unfavorably treat job candidates of Maghrebi origins. Their study was based on last and first names on CVs as proxies for race. Additionally, French demographer Dominique Meurs published the results of a 2017 survey that indicate that immigrants and their descendants are more often unemployed than the majority population, and these high levels of unemployment are not explained by their socioeconomic status (age, educational level). Furthermore, using the TeO survey dataset allowed Meurs (2017) to show a correspondence between respondents' reported experience of unfair treatment linked to origin and skin color, among other factors, and the objective measures of job discrimination in their current situation. In other words, qualitative data are complementary to and consistent with quantitative data.

Finally, a 2019 study (Athari et al, 2019) claims that immigrants and descendants of immigrants in France, particularly those with origins in the Maghreb and sub-Saharan Africa, experience difficulties and discrimination with regard to employment, notably in terms of access to jobs and salary levels.

Thus one of the ways in which we see colorblind racism operating is in the job market and the workplace. Since France does not allow explicitly for the measurement of racial categories, it is difficult to assess racial discrimination in the workforce. According to Véronique de Rudder and François Vourc'h (2009), one of the issues in the workplace is that it presents itself, particularly in the private sector, as a world led by economic rationality. Without data, claims of discrimination by individuals and groups are denied and considered as irrational and counter-productive in a place that is presented as colorblind and driven by supposedly neutral policies and expectations such as efficiency and productivity. As Bonilla-Silva (2006) explains, such colorblind rationalizations allow unequal treatment to be framed in abstract terms that seem neutral and void of any racial and racist implications.

At the same time, that companies and administrations in France are attempting to manage more diverse workforces, is in a way an admission that racial inequalities do exist in the workplace, which would contradict a colorblind perspective. Indeed, Claude Bébéar (2004: 17) claims that "discrimination exists at all levels in companies" and that the state should force companies to modify their hiring and promotion practices. In fact, in 2004, the Montaigne Institute (a French transpartisan think tank based in Paris that issues public policy recommendations) initiated a Chart of Diversity to encourage companies to engage with their practices in favor of social, cultural, and ethnic diversity. By 2017, more than 3,000 companies and nonprofit organizations had signed the chart (Masclet, 2017). However, Bereni (2009) observes that certain terms in the chart have been systematically eliminated, such as "equality," "fight against," "right," and "racism," and have been replaced by other terms like "proactive policies" or "strategic policies." Bereni (2009) also notes that whereas the term diversity was initially used mainly to refer to racial discrimination, it later became a generic category that includes all forms of discrimination (sex, age, physical abilities). The implication is that there is no need for a particular focus on racial discrimination and that the diversity measures are applied *à la carte*, case by case, at the individual level. De Rudder and Vourc'h (2009) confirm that the notions of institutional or systemic racism became absent.

Education discrimination

As noted by Fabrice Dhume (2013), the concept of racial discrimination in French school was first used in the scientific literature in the late 1970s, specifically in an article about the school orientation of immigrants' children published by French sociologist J.P. Zirotti in 1978. Previously, it was only in the 1960s that French social science research became interested in the place of immigration in the French school system (Dhume, 2013). At that point, researchers focused on specific questions – learning French as a second language, for example – and themes related to what were perceived to be problems (for example, "cultural distance," adaptation issues, school failure). So the research at that time was centered on the question of integration in school for the children of immigrants, not racial minority discrimination.

It was only in the mid-1970s that some research articles unveiled evidence of bias in grading students according to their national origin, of a pattern of medicalization of school failure for children of immigrants, and even a pattern of nonverbal communication from teachers projecting attraction/repulsion toward students according to their social class or national origin (Dhume, 2013). But these articles do not mention the term discrimination. In the 1980s and 1990s, only a few research studies focused on patterns of ethnic segregation at school. For example, Abdelmalek Sayad explored some of the disadvantages and inequality in treatment experienced at school by children with immigrant parents from the Maghreb. However, according to Dhume (2013), it was only in the aftermath of the 2005 ethnic riots that the idea of school discrimination on the basis of race and ethnicity would really emerge.

Second, as previously noted, one of the methodological issues involved in measuring racial discrimination is the absence of racial categories. In a study, Yaël Brinbaum et al (2012) indicate that they are examining the academic career of students residing in France who are children of immigrants compared with students who are not the children of immigrant parents nor immigrants themselves. They define "children of immigrants" as belonging to two different categories of population: (1) children born in France of one or two immigrant parents (that is, at least one parent is foreign-born); and (2) immigrant children of foreign origin who are considered as immigrants because they are foreigners born abroad. In this case, we are not able to differentiate between immigrants and French racial minorities. Similarly, Dhume (2013) explains that one of the issues affecting research in the 1970s was the need to develop categories that would adequately represent the diversity of ethnic backgrounds. At the time, Zirotti (1989) chose the notion of ETI or "enfants de travailleurs immigrés" (children of immigrant workers), and he then chose the terminology of "Maghrébins" (North Africans).

Therefore, once again, due to the impossibility of collecting racial data in France, most of the studies examining the issue of ethnic and racial discrimination in French schools resort to categories such as foreigners, descendants of immigrants, children of immigrants, and grandchildren of immigrants as proxies for race but lump them into a singular category that does not reflect the diversity of their statuses. Indeed, Georges Felouzis et al (2015) remark that because some information is considered sensitive by French law, it is impossible to access specific types of data. For example, surveys of French students cannot indicate their spoken language (other than French), their parents' birthplace, or the birthplace of first-generation students. This is problematic for scholars attempting to examine French students' school performance and achievement, particularly with international surveys like the Program for International Student Assessment (PISA, an international study carried out by OECD members to measure students' performance in mathematics, science, and reading). In fact, France is one of the few countries among the PISA survey's 65 participants to mask such information – language, birthplace, and so on – which makes it impossible to analyze inequality in school performance since the data doesn't show any differences in individual statuses.

In their study comparing the academic career of children of immigrants, Brinbaum et al (2012) explain that the success rate can be measured with two indicators: not having received any qualifications between elementary school and high school on the one hand, and having received a high school diploma on the other. With these two criteria in mind, Brinbaum et al (2012) show that the academic career and success of children of immigrant parents differ according to their parents' country of birth. For example, children whose parents are from Turkey, Algeria, Spain, or Italy are overrepresented in the category of individuals who did not receive any kind of degree between elementary school and high school.

In her research article on the academic career of the grandchildren of immigrants and their aspirations in higher education, Pauline Vallot (2016) shows that the grandchildren of immigrants graduating from high school in France have had less desire to pursue studies in higher education than children of immigrants, and less than children of parents from the majority population.

Similarly, in their study on the school performance of immigrant descendants, Felouzis et al (2015) show an increase in inequality for descendants of immigrants in terms of knowledge acquisition at all levels from elementary school to the end of high school compared with the majority population (as previously defined). Felouzis et al (2015) explain that there have been two explanations for this education gap: (1) that cultural discontinuity between family socialization and school expectations and norms is the primary source of inequalities in terms of experience, learning, and overall academic career; and (2) that the disadvantages these populations face mainly come from their lower socioeconomic background, which means they are more disenfranchised, and because school is indifferent to differences and therefore reproduces inequalities. This second framework has been the long-preferred explanation in France.

From these two arguments follow two hypotheses that could explain the sort of glass ceiling that limits the acquired knowledge and competencies of non-native students: one is that non-native students employ different school strategies (to study for example) due to cultural differences according to their national origins, while the second is that they have different sets of family values and practices that are not the ones promoted by the school system, which prevents them from succeeding at the same rate as native French students, despite French school presumably being indifferent to differences. The idea that French schools are indifferent to differences comes from the ideal presented by the French education system, which portrays itself as the school of the Republic and promotes equal opportunities for all by offering the same teaching to everyone equally. However, Felouzis et al (2015) argue that this premise represents an ideal rather than the reality of how the French school system works in practice. For example, segregation takes place because of the way the school is set up in terms of a hierarchy in the curriculum for majors and minors, which has consequences for the quality of the teaching. As demonstrated by Pierre Merle's (2012) study on school expenses, this implies that privileged students from a higher socioeconomic status receive the best education conditions, with the most experienced teachers and the best classroom equipment and general classroom resources. Thus we are not in the context of a school that's indifferent to differences but rather in a context where school produces inequalities through systemic discrimination connected to urban, social, and educational factors. These factors have in fact increased the cultural distancing (or discontinuity) between non-native students and the school system.

The second hypothesis defended by Felouzis et al (2015) is that systemic discrimination is linked to the learning environment of non-native students, as they tend to be concentrated in the same high schools. In this case, systemic discrimination does not necessarily imply an explicit and conscious intention. Simon and Stavo-Debauge explain that "systemic discrimination can be observed outside of its intentionality, and it can be comprehended essentially in the effects and consequences of a treatment. It will be considered discriminatory if it affects systematically, negatively, and disproportionately, individuals from a given group" (2004: 62). As Felouzis et al (2015) demonstrate, research shows that the social segregation of the schools in disenfranchised neighborhoods produces inequalities in terms of the learning conditions, the level of resources available in a school, the quality of the teaching, the seniority and experience of teachers, the high turnover of the teaching staff, and the kinds of pedagogical practices in place all represent powerful factors producing educational inequalities for non-native students. Thus, as noted by Dhume (2013), contrary to the previous assertion by some social scientists that French school integrates and does not discriminate, the aforementioned effects and consequences showing inequalities in school constitute systemic discrimination against non-native students.

Yet, some French social scientists continue to claim that race is not a factor of discrimination, even though studies have revealed inequalities between racial minority students and majority students in France. For example, in her article on the higher education aspirations of grandchildren and children of immigrants, Vallot (2016) takes into consideration migration history and socioeconomic status but without accounting for race or ethnicity. In fact, Vallot (2016) concludes that American sociology's focus on racial discrimination does not apply to her research in the French context. Indeed, since three quarters of the population she surveyed is composed of students of a European immigrant background, she argues that such a focus is not relevant for analyzing patterns of discrimination in terms of ethnicity or race. Vallot (2016) seems to deny the salience of race while at the same time acknowledging it. On the one hand, she attempts to dismiss the role played by race and ethnicity in academic inequalities and instead solely focuses on the immigration history and the socioeconomic status of the students. Yet, on the other hand, she argues that the surveyed population wouldn't have experienced racial discrimination because they have a European immigration background, which implies they are not a racial minority, that they perhaps have no race, and/or that they are White because they are Europeans and as such are not affected by racial discrimination. In some ways, it is as if she is both dismissing and admitting to the significance of race, which seems to correspond to one of the colorblind racism frames developed by Bonilla-Silva (2006): the minimization of racism, whereby racial discrimination is not considered a central factor affecting the life chances of racial minorities.

Most of the research on education ultimately shows that inequalities in competency, academic achievement, academic performance, and career aspirations between native students and non–native students in France have increased since the early 2000s. However, on the one hand, most of these studies are framed in terms of first- and second-generation immigrants rather than racial minorities due to the impossibility of including racial categories, and thus, this does not reflect accurately the diversity, complexity, and nuances in the status and conditions of all French citizens. In other words, due to a methodological and epistemological impasse, the impression given by these studies is that the population in France is divided into two parts: a majority native population that is relatively successful, and an immigrant population, which includes the descendants of immigrants, that is experiencing issues in terms of achievement and success. On the other hand, because these studies rely on data about the immigrant population, their focus and arguments remain centered on the question of integration. That is, the results are often analyzed in terms of how well integrated children of immigrants are into mainstream or majority French society rather than examining the mechanisms in the reproduction of inequalities, direct or indirect, that the French education system uses to the detriment of both French racial minorities and immigrant populations.

Residential segregation

According to Patrick Weil (2005), the educational achievement of children born in France of North African and sub-Saharan African origins is negatively affected by residential segregation and poor housing conditions. As Castel (2007) explains, even with higher education degrees, children from immigrant families experience a form of glass ceiling that reduces the likelihood of them being hired and/or promoted. Additionally, for Edo and Jacquement (2013), one of the significant consequences of employment discrimination is to reinforce and maintain spatial segregation, which leads to the concentration of populations of immigrant descent in confined geographical zones.

As Michel Kokoreff (2009) notes, since the mid-1980s a significant number of publications in French sociology have focused on the inequalities in France's "banlieues" (suburbs). Kokoreff (2009) explains that some sociologists have focused specifically on the social difficulties accumulated in these outsider urban spaces while rejecting any comparison with the American sociological approach to racial residential segregation. Other sociologists, while recognizing the specificities of different structures and contexts in France and the United States, still underline some of the similarities between the two societies in terms of the structural processes that negatively affect certain ethnic groups over others.

Although there has been a more significant amount of literature on racial discrimination and its effects on residential mobility in the US compared with France, François Bonnet et al (2015) note that the body of research studies documenting ethnic segregation is growing in France. However, it is challenging for research scientists to collect relevant data because of the republican model and its colorblind universalist model of citizenship, which denies ethnic/racial identification and fails to collect ethno-racial statistics. Nonetheless, as seen with research in education discrimination, in the aftermath of the 2005 ethnic riots an increasing number of studies have highlighted the racial dimension of inequalities in French society.

In their study on the difficulties immigrants and their descendants face in accessing housing in France, Jean-Louis Pan Ké Shon and Claire Scodellaro (2011) explain that different levels of discrimination are at work. They define direct racial discrimination as a

> situation in which, on the foundation of one's membership or non-membership, real or presumed, of an ethnic group or a race, one's religion, one's convictions, one's age, one's handicap, one's sexual orientation or one's sex, a person is treated more or less favorably than another person in a similar situation. (Pan Ké Shon and Scodellaro, 2011: 3; as cited in French law of adaptation to the European Union law no. 2008–496)

Indirect racial discrimination rests on "a disposition, a criteria, or a practice in appearance neutral, but susceptible to provoke … a particular disadvantage for some people compared with others" (French law of adaptation to the European Union law no. 2008-496).

Pan Ké Shon and Scodellaro define segregation as the "concentration of disenfranchised populations in enclosed spaces" (2011: 4), which goes with the idea of being put in the margins, as well as receiving punitive and unequal treatment. They explain that segregation takes place on a continuum with many degrees of intensity corresponding to different social situations.

First, Pan Ké Shon and Scodellaro (2018) point to a diversity of types of residential areas in France with a White rural habitat on the one hand – White being the term used by the authors, which is unusual for French social scientists – and multi-ethnic as well as segregated urban areas that are often disenfranchised on the other hand. Their study measures the spatial concentration of immigrant populations at different socio-spatial levels: according to the proportion of low-cost public housing (Habitation à Loyers Modérés), unemployment rate, and immigrant population rate.

In their study on the living environment of immigrants and their descendants, Pan Ké Shon and Scodellaro (2018) show that immigrants in France disproportionately reside in disenfranchised neighborhoods, with concentration levels that differ according to their inhabitants' origins. For example, sub-Saharan African and North African immigrants mostly live in densely populated areas. Another finding of the study is that what is called the majority population is grouped in the wealthy neighborhoods, middle-class/lower socio-economic status neighborhoods, and tend to avoid disenfranchised neighborhoods.

Although Pan Ké Shon and Scodellaro (2018) state that housing discrimination in France seems relatively limited (with 9 percent for sub-Saharan Africans and North Africans meaning that according to data, only 9 percent of sub-Saharan Africans and North Africans residing in France report having experienced housing discrimination), they point out that these numbers are probably under-estimated and underreported by those who are affected. Indeed, Pan Ké Shon and Scodellaro (2018) argue that for French social scientists, one of the issues in examining residential segregation on the basis of race and ethnicity is to be able to distinguish between what they call perceived and objective segregation. They explain that it is necessary to take into account variables such as gender, age, national origin, and type of residence (for example, public housing) that may influence a person's perception and response toward the proportion of immigrants living in the neighborhood. In this sense, contrary to what some other French social scientists have claimed, race is a significant factor when it comes to the perception of residential segregation, which is what Pan Ké Shon and Scodellaro (2018) examine in their research. The authors explain that when asked to identify who they think the residents in their neighborhoods are, individuals interviewed in the survey sometimes conflate the notion of "immigrant" with foreigner, sometimes include descendants of immigrants, and sometimes extend the category to anyone they think possesses characteristics perceived as connected to that of immigrants. In a separate essay, Pan Ké Shon (2010) argues that if social class segregation has decreased, ethno-racial segregation has increased. In order to evaluate such segregation patterns, it is important to distinguish the diversity of communities who are subjected to different levels of intensity of discrimination according to their history or their physical appearance.

Furthermore, discrimination is targeted primarily against African communities, whether sub-Saharan African or North African immigrants, whereas European immigrants have to some extent become invisible. Also, despite high levels of discrimination leading to housing segregation for African immigrants in disenfranchised urban areas, residents are not entirely locked-in, and they do experience residential mobility, albeit not necessarily upward mobility.

Pan Ké Shon (2011) shows that Maghrebi, sub-Saharan Africans, Turks, and Asians represent the immigrant populations most affected by spatial segregation. In the 1990s, that situation deteriorated for Turks, Algerians, and Moroccans. A 2008 TeO survey conducted by INED shows that 42 percent of immigrants from Africa, Maghreb, and Turkey reside in the 10 percent of neighborhoods with the highest rates of unemployment. They also comprise 28 percent of the population residing in disenfranchised neighborhoods (called in French the Zones Urbaines Sensibles [ZUS], or more commonly "quartiers sensibles," "sensitive neighborhoods"). In his study on residential segregation, Pan Ké Shon (2011) notes that the persistence in overrepresentation of immigrants and their children in low-income communities seems to indicate that several factors are at play in terms of population segregation: low-rent housing and concentration of social housing, as well as direct or indirect employment discrimination.

More specifically, immigrants are concentrated in the lower socioeconomic status neighborhoods and the disenfranchised neighborhoods, whereas descendants of immigrants are more dispersed on the socio-spatial territory: they tend to reside more frequently in the middle-class/lower socioeconomic status neighborhoods than their parents. However, residential integration can be observed over generations in the sense that there is an ascending residential mobility for the descendants of immigrants. And yet, at the same time, Pan Ké Shon and Scodellaro (2011) observe a frequent pattern of descending mobility for sub-Saharan African, North African, and Turkish immigrants and descendants of immigrants as compared with the majority population. This double movement of ascending and descending residential mobility for immigrants and their descendants shows that the residential segregation patterns are diverse and relate more to the idea of ethnic clusters than ghettos, according to Pan Ké Shon and Scodellaro (2011). In this sense, Pan Ké Shon (2011) notes, residential mobility is actually high in these particular segregated neighborhoods, which seems to indicate a trend toward what he calls residential integration in the long term.

In his study, Pan Ké Shon (2010) found that the housing trajectories of African immigrants present a *trend*: some of the African immigrants moved out of the ZUS areas into neighborhoods with less insecure employment, although residential mobility is harder to achieve for them than for other immigrant groups or other groups from the majority population.

Similarly, Bonnet et al's (2015) study shows the difficulties racial minorities face when accessing housing in France. Their study stems from two observations about gaps in the research: (1) there is no real study-based evidence in France of housing discrimination, hence the need to examine ethnic discrimination in the Paris housing market; and (2) there is a need to examine the interconnection between ethnic disadvantage (specifically for individuals of North African background) and territorial discrimination, which may undermine residential mobility out of the *banlieues*.

Using testing and interviews with real estate agents, Bonnet et al (2015) pose two hypotheses, the first of which is that residential segregation could be due to statistical discrimination, that is, the phenomenon where real estate agents include the risk of nonpayment of the rent using criteria like residential origin and use the characteristics they attribute to that particular criteria to infer a risk of nonpayment. The authors say that this kind of disadvantage may appear colorblind because race isn't explicitly used (it is the residential origin instead that is explicitly designated), but it is in fact a driving factor for housing discrimination along with socioeconomic factors. Their second hypothesis is that residential segregation might be due to an ethnic stigma as the predominant factor, whereas residential origin has no direct relevance and is only used as a proxy for race/ethnicity. However, the way of using proxies is also indicative of the level of discrimination in the housing search process: indeed, real estate agents might not use names as factors to discriminate because they perceive it as too obvious a proxy for race or ethnicity but will be more comfortable using residential origin to discriminate because it is more ambivalent and not seen as a proxy for race, and therefore not perceived as discriminatory, even though it is.

Additionally, housing discrimination based on directly racist motives, such as skin color, origin, and nationality, as declared by the respondents, amounts to 9.4 percent for sub-Saharan African and North African immigrants and 6.3 percent for their descendants, as opposed to 0.4 percent for immigrants and their descendants of other origins. Pan Ké Shon and Scodellaro (2011) state that racial discrimination is probably underreported and under-evaluated in part because they mostly concern direct discrimination, and that more statistical research could highlight patterns of indirect discrimination.

McAvay (2017) confirms what other research studies have shown, namely that there are patterns of spatial clustering among immigrant populations from Africa. However, contrary to the findings of Pan Ké Shon (2010), the author observes that there are significant similarities between first- and second-generation (their descendants) immigrants in terms of spatial segregation: that is, the descendants of immigrants do not seem to show an increase in spatial assimilation, and thus ethnic clustering is not weaker, which of course tends to reinforce the common trope in France that immigrants choose to cluster together.

But for McAvay (2017), one of the explanations for patterns of ethno-racial segmentation in the housing market is that postcolonial immigrants in France have been limited in their choices of housing and encouraged to pursue public housing in the *banlieues*. These neighborhoods later experienced socioeconomic disadvantages such as higher levels of unemployment and poor quality education and resources that have prevented these immigrant populations from moving out and upwards.

In conclusion, residential segregation tends to affect more sub-Saharan African, North African, and Turkish immigrants and their descendants, especially those who live in the ZUS and the Zones Franches Urbaines (ZFU, or Urban Tax-free zones), than members of the majority population. Indeed, Pan Ké Shon and Scodellaro (2011) explain that their study shows a statistical overrepresentation of sub-Saharan African, North African, and Turkish immigrants in the most disadvantaged urban areas, in the margins of cities, such as ZUS and ZFU.

Public housing, located in these urban areas, represents more than half of the residence of immigrants from sub-Saharan Africa, North Africa, and Turkey. Besides their lower socioeconomic status, which prevents them from residential mobility out of public housing and out of these particular urban areas, Pan Ké Shon and Scodellaro (2011) also argue that a significant factor is the direct or indirect discrimination in the private housing sector that immigrants and descendants of immigrants experience, which precludes them from residential mobility. Thus, segregation can take place because of individual choices or institutional decisions, for example the attribution of the least desirable public housing to sub-Saharan African immigrants or North African immigrants specifically, which produces discrimination and direct segregation of these populations.

As seen previously, one of the negative consequences of residential segregation is the impact it has on education for the descendants of immigrants, who are limited to accessing schools offering lower quality education (Piketty and Valdenaire, 2006). This consequently results in the reproduction of inequalities and the reduction of possible choices for children (Maurin, 2004), as well as in individually self-destructive behavioral patterns (Pan Ké Shon, 2009).

Compared with the United States, France seems to avoid discussions about the segregation of some of its inhabitants. Pan Ké Shon and Scodellaro (2011) argue that the fight against racial discrimination in housing is still a blind spot in French society. The French republican ideal based on the three principles of liberty, equality, fraternity, Pan Ké Shon (2010) says, is also imaginary and not representative of the lives of racial minorities in France who experience spatial concentration, poverty, and discrimination. The 2005 ethnic riots brought a repressed reality back into the picture.

However, McAvay (2017) claims that since 2010 there has been more focus on, and more public debates in France geared toward, urban inequalities as they are impacting the immigrant populations and their descendants. That being said, residential segregation is often associated with socioeconomic disadvantage, high unemployment, crime, poor school quality, and poor public housing. This is often framed as the inability and refusal of immigrant populations from Africa to integrate into mainstream France.

In the end, the conclusion is that ethnic segregation in France results from a combination of factors, including the more frequent channeling, by French institutions and the real estate sector, of incoming African immigrants toward sensitive neighborhoods (such as ZUS or ZFU) and the specific challenges that African immigrants face in attempting to achieve residential mobility and upward mobility. As underlined by Pan Ké Shon (2010), some of the additional issues are that (1) because France does not officially recognize race as a demographic category, it does not have any proactive policies that would recognize and specifically address ethnic discrimination in housing, not just among immigrants but also French racial minorities; and (2) there has been a shift in government policies toward the *banlieues*, with more repression against racial minorities (including immigrant communities) on the one hand and less assistance and government funding for comprehensive urban renovation in the *banlieues* on the other.

Race and policing

Thierry Delpeuch et al (2017) note that sociologists in the United States started studying police brutality in the 1960s, as racism and police violence were initiating factors in some of the urban riots that took place between 1964 and 1968. In France, Fabien Jobard and Omar Slaouti (2020) explain that social scientist René Lévy began to show evidence in the 1970s and 1980s that the decision of the Parisian police to arrest and bring individuals to court was in great part determined by ethno-racial considerations, meaning that individuals perceived as African or North African were arrested more frequently than members of the majority population.

More than 40 years later, in 2016 the Defender of Rights demonstrated that young Black and Arab men are five times more likely to be "controlled" (subject to ID checks) by the police than other young men in French society.

In the same year, the highest court in the French judiciary, the Court of Cassation, established that every year the millions of ID controls operated by the police fell under discrimination law because of the overrepresentation of young men of color among the population that was checked by police forces (Court de Cassation, November 9, 2016).

In its 2019 decision (Decision 2019-090, April 2, 2019), the Defender of Rights claims that police practices amount to "racial and social profiling" during ID controls. Specifically, the Defender of Rights (Decision 2019–090, April 2, 2019) declares that "discriminatory orders and instructions inviting [police] to proceed to ID control of groups of Black people and North Africans, and to evict homeless individuals and Roms, have been released."

More recently, on December 4, 2020, French President Macron admitted in an interview with online news website Brut that "today, when a person has a skin color that is not White, they are controlled much more ... They are identified as a factor of a problem and that's unbearable."

Compared with the rest of Europe, ID controls occupy a more significant place in police work in France despite such checks not being among the essential functions of a police officer.

In their research, Jobard and Slaouti (2020) show that the actions of the police forces are part of an institutional racism, that is, a series of decisions and provisions, which, through their implementation and accumulation, produces differential and illegal treatment based on a person's origins or presumed origins.

However, Jobard and Slaouti (2020) explain that, for French institutions, the expression systemic discrimination is actually a new term. The idea that the actions of the police essentially rest on a system of structural inequality in treatment based on skin color has been very slow to be taken into consideration by the highest institutions of the judiciary. It took many studies and reports by the different courts of the French judiciary to highlight what many victims of abuse and abusive controls by the police have experienced daily. These realities have been denounced for a long time by several human rights and civil rights organizations fighting against police violence in France: Mouvement de l'Immigration et des Banlieues, Collectif Urgence Notre Police Assassine, L'Observatoire Nationale des Violences Policières, le Collectif Vies Volées, and Collectif pour Adama. Furthermore, the French state has been reprimanded several times by the European Court of Human Rights for the police's use of a tackling method called "technique du pliage" or "folding technique" against individuals that results in serious harm and sometimes death (Jobard and Slaouti, 2020).

French historian Emmanuel Blanchard (2014) argues that ID controls are more than just a police action – they are a political action in the sense that checking someone's ID without probable cause for anything is a way to deny the legitimacy of a person's presence and condition. Blanchard (2014) equates this action to Harold Garfinkel's concept of "degradation ceremony" (1956), that is, a ceremony that is intended to transform a person's identity or status into a lower status within the hierarchy of a group or institution. These degradation ceremonies can take different forms and modalities: for example, using the familiar "tu" in French to address a person (equivalent to calling someone by their first name instead of a formal address such as Mr.), the use of insults, or even the use of brutality. This form of degradation primarily impacts those who already experience racial discrimination in other sectors of society.

Jobard and Slaouti (2020) explain that France has created police forces specially trained to operate in the disenfranchised neighborhoods in the *banlieues*: the Brigades Spécialisées de Terrain (BST, or Field Special Brigades), which were created in 2008, shortly after the 2005 ethnic riots in the northern *banlieues* of Paris; and the Brigade Anti-Criminalité (BAC, or Anti-Criminality Brigade), created in 1994, which is mostly present in Paris and its *banlieues* with specialized day- and night-units. Didier Fassin's research (2011) reveals the political radicalization of these types of brigades, with co-optation and affinities with extreme right ideas. René Lévy and Renée Zauberman (1998) have made similar observations: fieldwork studies conclude that there is a generalized racist discourse within the police that constitutes a norm against which it is hard to fight or oppose. Today, many studies have unveiled the mechanisms of production of systemic repressive police harassment against immigrants and their descendants.

However, Jobard and Slaouti (2020) argue that individual racism and institutional racism are not distinct categories of what is taking place in the police forces: according to Jobard and Slaouti (2020), institutional racism provides the conditions of emergence, expressions, and justifications of personal racism in police forces. The ID controls that are a central part of the production and reproduction of institutional racism within the judicial system are performed by police forces within the confines of the law and under the authority of France's Attorney General. Thus, it is the judiciary itself that sanctions a logic of racialization of urban spaces and of criminalization of immigrants and their descendants in France, despite the official claim of the republican model's colorblindness. In this sense, Jobard and Slaouti (2020) argue, based on empirical data, the notion of "state racism" is relevant in the French case, since it is indeed under the authority of the French judiciary that decisions, measures, and practices operated by the police over the entire French territory systematically target certain groups among the entire population.

Blanchard (2018) shows that for oppressed groups of young Black and Arab men in France, there is a link between current police practices and France's colonial past. That is, the same policies and practices that sustained and perpetuated colonial domination are currently being applied against racial minority populations in France. In fact, the specialized police brigades currently in place in the disenfranchised *banlieues* of Paris are reminiscent of colonial administrative institutions. For example, from 1925 until 1945, the municipality of Paris had put in place the Service de surveillance et de protection des Nord-Africains (SSPNA, or Service of Protection and Surveillance of North Africans), sometimes called Brigade Nord-Africaine, which was the central office of political and administrative control of Algerians residing in France. Today, there are similar patterns of law and order measures specifically targeting certain disenfranchised and marginalized territories where populations of color reside (particularly immigrants from former French colonies). For example, in 2008 the Minister of Interior set up a program called "Quartiers de Reconquête Républicaine" (or "Neighborhoods of Republican Recapture"), which are still in place today and were presented as a set of measures for daily security and order involving police presence and actions to fight against delinquency and trafficking, though targeting only certain neighborhoods in major French cities (the Parisian suburbs, Marseille, Lyon, and Lille, for example), which also happen to be disenfranchised, with high poverty rates, high levels of unemployment, and where most of the immigrant and racial minority populations reside. Jobard and Slaouti (2020) view this moral and belligerent rhetoric as manifesting a form of continuity with colonial practices toward populations from former French colonies. As a result of this systematic racial targeting and profiling, for young men of color in France unjustified encounters with the police (for an ID check, for example) are far more frequent than for all other groups of the population and their consequences far more grave and damaging. For Jobard and Slaouti (2020), that the French state does not denounce or condemn state racism is significant because such denial and avoidance participate in the reproduction of a colorblind racism at the heart of French society. This is supported by systemic racism's reliance on a legal apparatus that is supported by the political elite, including elected officials, representatives, and government officials.

For French social scientist Mathieu Rigouste (2011), the opposition between the republican order and what is constructed as "false French" citizens emerged in the 1980s, with the creation of the figure of the "second-generation" immigrant/French, and "French from an immigrant/ immigration background" (or "Français issus de l'immigration") in the media and among the political elite. According to Rigouste (2011), this nonlegal category targeted the children of postcolonial immigrants, particularly from the Maghreb, and as underlined by the author, basically nonWhite populations. These kinds of categorizations enabled immigration terms to be used as proxies for the notion of race, operating a symbolic division between supposed "real" French and "false" French citizens, who are then viewed as suspicious with regard to their allegiance to France. Rigouste (2011) argues that it was also during that time that the French *banlieues*, where immigrant populations are often concentrated, started to be described and designated as "sensible" urban territories, conflating them with dangerous criminal spaces left to populations who are unable to integrate into French society. Also called sensitive urban zones (Zones Urbaines Sensibles), they are defined by the French administration as urban areas that are high priority targets in terms of public policies, due to their difficult socio-economic status (high percentage of public housing, high unemployment rate, low percentage of high school graduates). The idea behind this kind of discourse, supported by the media and the political elite, was to convince the broader population that the "second generation" was a threat to the "real" French identity ("la menace identitaire") and that the state needed to reestablish law and order against this "internal postcolonial enemy" (Rigouste, 2011: 189). According to Rigouste (2011), it is with this idea of the preservation of national identity in postcolonial times that we should analyze the deployment of special police forces in the French *banlieues* operating racial profiling and committing state-endorsed violence against racial minorities.

Similarly, according to the Observatoire des Inégalités (2021), a survey conducted by the Defender of Rights in 2016 shows that 22 percent of men who self-identify as Arab and 13 percent of men who self-identify as Black declare they have been controlled by the police more than five times in the past five years, which is ten times more than for White men. Controlling for other factors such as age and place of residence, the study shows that young men who self-identify as Arab or Black have a 19 percent higher likelihood of being controlled by the police than the rest of the population. One of the issues is that the neighborhoods where many immigrants and French racial minority populations reside are also disenfranchised, with high unemployment rates and other social injustices, such as fewer resources for education, for example. And these police control operations specifically targeting racial minorities seem to imply that a safety and order problem exists in the *banlieues*, hence the need for police control. And yet, as noted by the Observatoire des Inégalités (2021), the excessive police ID checks of racial minorities has not improved the security issues in these particular urban areas.

Finally, in their research into police discourse about racial minorities in different European countries, François Bonnet and Clothilde Caillault (2015) argue that racism in police speech can be conceptualized as a category of practice where different speech norms influence the discourse of the police. They observe that significant variations in speech norms exist between countries. For example, while French police officers seem to respect strict speech norms, Dutch and Italian officers apparently use language that might be considered shocking in anglophone societies. Bonnet and Caillault (2015) argue that one of the reasons for this is that the national definition of what is considered racist varies greatly between countries, and thus more specific research is required to understand speech patterns. They conclude that while a society like France may have stricter speech norms in terms of nonracist speech compared with the Netherlands and Italy, this does not necessarily translate into nonracist policies, especially with regard to police interaction with racial minorities. In fact, recurring rioting in the *banlieues* of France is almost always incited by police brutality or police violence.

Health disparities

As noted by Marguerite Cognet (2020), the COVID-19 pandemic that started in March 2020 helped shed some light on the issue of health inequalities and discrimination in France. Studies on COVID-19 regarding the situation in the United States or the United Kingdom, both of which collect racial and ethnic statistics, have highlighted the overrepresentation of racial minorities among the victims of COVID-19. Concerning the pandemic situation in France, most of the media and political commentaries have noted the high mortality rate in the department of Seine-Saint-Denis, which is located northeast of Paris and is the French department with the highest proportion of immigrants. It is also disenfranchised economically, with high poverty and unemployment rates. However, French demographer Simon (2020) explains that these media reports only focus on that particular department of Seine-Saint-Denis. In the meantime, the statistics published by government organizations regarding the COVID-19 pandemic provide no information on the infection rates or the mortality rate of immigrants and descendants of immigrants in the rest of France. Unfortunately, as Simon (2020) shows, health statistics in general contain no information related to the origins of the individuals, and thus it is particularly challenging to draw any conclusions about the situation of racial minorities in France in terms of their health status during the COVID-19 pandemic. The only data available, published weekly by INSEE, are related to the death records of cities in each department of France. However, these death records take account of the place of death of the person rather than their place of residence.

Table 3.7 outlines the composition of the population of Seine-St-Denis.

Simon (2020) used different datasets to come up with relevant results, showing excess mortality rates (defined as abnormally high mortality rates

Table 3.7: Seine-St-Denis department immigrants and descendants of immigrants, 2020

Seine-St-Denis Department	Ile-de-France Region	France
30% of residents are immigrants	16.9% of residents are immigrants	10.2% of residents are immigrants
28% of adults 18 to 50 years old are descendants of immigrants	18% of adults 18 to 50 years old are descendants of immigrants	
50% of children less than 18 years old are descendants of immigrants	33% of children less than 18 years old are descendants of immigrants	

Source: Simon (2020)

Table 3.8: Excess death rates in the departments of Seine-St-Denis, Hauts-de-Seine, City of Paris, 2020

	Excess death rate March 1–April 19, 2020 (%)
Department of Seine-St-Denis	134
Department of Hauts-de-Seine	114
City of Paris	99

Source: Simon (2020)

compared with the expected mortality rate at the same time period). It emerges that the Seine-St-Denis department has the highest excess death rate in the region when compared with other departments (see Table 3.8).

Simon (2020) shows that most of the residents of Seine-St-Denis died in a hospital or private clinic (60 percent) instead of at home or in a nursing home as for other residents of wealthier departments. Simon (2020) details some of the factors explaining the high exposure rate of the population of the Seine-St-Denis to COVID-19:

- The department of Seine-St-Denis is the third most populous department after Paris and the Hauts-de-Seine department: population density is 6,802 inhabitants per km².
- In terms of housing conditions, the department of Seine-St-Denis has the highest rate of over-occupancy in the entire region of Ile-de-France, along with frequent multi-generation cohabitation, which might accelerate the transmission rate. Additionally, Seine-St-Denis has the highest number of migrant workers' group housing.
- The department of Seine-St-Denis' poverty rate is 29 percent (which is higher than other departments, like Yvelines at 10 percent, or Hauts-de-Seine at 12 percent), and the standard of living is the lowest in all of metropolitan France.
- The Seine-St-Denis department also has the highest use of public transportation to go to work (53 percent versus an average of 43 percent for the Ile-de-France region), which is also an important risk factor with regard to COVID-19 infection.
- Finally, in terms of health structures, equipment, and personnel: the department of Seine-St-Denis has the lowest number of doctors per inhabitant (with doctors being older than the average for the region and the rest of the country); it also has the lowest rate of hospital equipment in the region, whether in terms of general medicine, surgery, gynecology, or recovery.

In addition to these socioeconomic and structural factors, Simon (2020) shows that comorbidity issues associated with COVID-19 (like diabetes) are specifically linked to socioeconomic conditions as well as country of origin.

Similarly, in a scientific study published in a medical journal, Azria et al (2020) discuss data regarding the overexposure to COVID-19 of racial minorities in the United States and the UK. The authors argue that the higher comorbidity rates are linked to medical conditions such as diabetes or obesity that are prevalent among certain racial minority populations, but that these are also connected to living conditions as well, such as type of employment and housing. As was also the case in Simon's (2020) research, Azria et al's (2020) study also notes that there are inequalities in terms of mortality due to COVID-19 in France linked to the country of origin of individuals.

However, both Simon (2020) and the medical study mentioned earlier (Azria et al, 2020) underline that without appropriate data on the French population, they cannot really measure all the factors impacting the health risks of individuals. Indeed, they all argue that any discussion about the health conditions of racial minorities in the context of the pandemic in France is treated in the media or through studies operated by government agencies with euphemisms, for example by focusing on the department of Seine-St-Denis and the presence of immigrants. The medical study by Elie Azria et al (2020) even argues that while health research studies in the United States or the United Kingdom take into account racial statistics, and examine the role of racial discrimination in health disparities, France is hesitant to even consider the possibility that ethnic discrimination might be a factor in patterns of health inequality.

Azria et al (2020) argue that the excess death rates due to COVID-19 among particular populations and communities during the pandemic in France highlight the larger issue of racial discrimination in healthcare. Generally, racial minorities and other marginalized groups face multifaceted issues that can impact their health negatively. Rivenbark and Ichou (2020) explain that experiences of discrimination can impact a person's health directly in terms of physiological stress and indirectly in terms of behavioral responses. For example, with regard to health-related behaviors, studies report that experiences of discrimination can affect diet, exercise, sleep, and substance use. However, Rivenbark and Ichou (2020) note that a less examined behavior influenced by discrimination is the use of healthcare. Indeed, individuals who report experiences of discrimination are less likely to seek healthcare as they believe they might be exposed to more discrimination by doing so. Research findings in the United States show a link between discrimination in healthcare settings and the likelihood of individuals delaying or even forgoing care altogether (Rivenbark and Ichou, 2020). The French case is interesting for research scientists because, as

Table 3.9: Criteria of discrimination per the French Penal Code

General criteria of discrimination	Details
Criteria connected to the origin	Origin Physical appearance Last name True or supposed membership or non-membership of an ethnic group, a nation, a race Place of residence
Criteria connected to the health status	Health condition Disability Genetic characteristics
Criteria connected to personal convictions	Political opinions Union activities Religion (true or supposed membership or non-membership of a determined religion)
Criteria connected to gender and sex	Sex Pregnancy status Sexual orientation Sexual identity
Criteria connected to lifestyle	Family situation Personal morals
Criteria connected to age	–

Source: Penal Code, Article 225-1, modified by Law 2014-173, February 21, 2014, Article 15

explained previously, France does not allow or recognize ethnic and racial categories, and thus racial statistics are not collected in the census and other official studies. Moreover, as France has a compulsory and universal health insurance coverage system for all of its residents, everyone in France should have relatively easy access to healthcare at very low or no out-of-pocket expense. In their study on discrimination in healthcare in the French region of Alsace, Emily Jung and Gaëlle Donnard (2016) note that the French code of public health (Article 1110-3, 2018) clearly states that "no one can be the object of discrimination in accessing preventive or health care. A health care professional cannot refuse to treat a person because of one of the motives" that are listed in the Penal Code.

The list of criteria considered by the French Penal Code as discriminating against the person are set out in Table 3.9.

In addition to the criteria listed in the Penal Code, the code of public health adds that being the recipient of universal health insurance and other social benefits usually granted to lower socioeconomic status individuals should not be a discriminating factor either. With all these legal protections and safeguards, and the French context of colorblindness, we might expect to find minimal racial discrimination in healthcare. And yet, the pandemic statistics have revealed that there are great disparities between neighborhoods, communities, departments, and regions based on both social class and race. In fact, despite a public healthcare program funded by the state, racial minorities in France do experience discrimination within the healthcare system. Not only are racial minorities not counted in the census but they are also not taken into consideration in terms of social policies with regard to healthcare (Rivenbark and Ichou, 2020).

Nonetheless, the overall conclusion based on current data (with data on first- and second-generation immigrants) suggests that discrimination experienced by racial minorities in France is in fact connected with foregoing healthcare (Rivenbark and Ichou, 2020). More specifically, three main findings emerge from the data used by Rivenbark and Ichou (2020): first, disenfranchised groups, such as racial minorities, are more likely to experience discrimination in healthcare settings, particularly immigrants and their children from sub-Saharan Africa and North Africa. Second, groups reporting higher rates of discrimination in healthcare settings are also more likely to forgo medical care. However, in the case of France, the conclusion from the findings differs from studies in the United States. Indeed, contrary to the US context, second-generation immigrants in France report higher rates of foregoing medical care than first-generation immigrants, which is the opposite of the United States. Third, all of these findings are consistent with existing research on the link between discrimination and healthcare use. It is also consistent with studies showing that the same immigrant populations experiencing discrimination in the healthcare system already face greater levels of racism within French society.

For Azria et al (2020), there is no doubt that the inequalities in access to healthcare are connected to race and social class. For them, economic, racial, and medical factors are all interconnected. In other words, racial discrimination is in fact a barrier to accessing proper healthcare. For Simon (2020), being able to include race and ethnicity in the data collection of COVID-19 patients would allow research scientists to better understand the pandemic and its effects on specific populations, as well as the effects of racial inequalities on healthcare in general. Estelle Carde (2011) echoes this idea and argues that, despite criticisms of and concerns about the collection of ethnic statistics, many French medical professionals regret that ethnic data are not collected. Carde (2011) adds that such ethnic categories are already used in epidemiological studies. Furthermore, Rivenbark and Ichou (2020) suggest recommendations to reduce discrimination in healthcare settings including a psychology research-based intervention at the provider level to improve understanding of bias and "increase perspective-taking and empathetic behaviors" (Rivenbark and Ichou, 2020: 29). For example, such intervention could include feedback on biased behaviors and interactions to reduce racial bias in prescribing pain medicine. In addition to changes with individual interaction settings between healthcare professionals and patients, more systemic interventions include better organizational accountability for discrimination. Generally, as argued by Carde (2011), including better measurement and examination of the barriers to medical care that racial minorities face within the healthcare system and healthcare settings would legitimize the application of policies targeting objective discrimination.

Conclusion

In conclusion to this chapter, the absence of racial categories forces researchers to resort to using proxies and/or euphemisms when examining racism and unfair treatment based on race in France. These are methodologically and epistemologically problematic for the reasons exposed in the chapter. By willfully ignoring the existence of race, and denying the possibility of using racial categories, colorblind policies end up reinforcing patterns of racial discrimination and segregation. They do so in three ways. First, because such policies deny the opportunity for social scientists to accurately collect evidence that would undeniably show patterns of discrimination based on race. Second, because colorblind policies fail to acknowledge the experience of those who suffer from patterns of discrimination, which makes them feel that their perception is subjective and exaggerated and cannot be verified scientifically. And third, colorblind policies keep discriminatory patterns under the radar without precise data and thus maintains the pretense that French society is colorblind and has no need to address issues that are not proven to be significant.

The French system of colorblind policies reveals the suspicion and constant shadow of doubt that racial minorities in France experience in terms of their Frenchness, in terms of their allegiance or loyalty to France, and in terms of the acknowledgment of their reality in facing racism. In the end, there is being French and looking French, and what isn't openly acknowledged through the use of proxies in these studies is that being French, sounding French, and looking French in contemporary France ultimately means being White.

On the other hand, it also shows both the limits and contradictions of a colorblind system in terms of the framing of the law, as contemporary French law excludes the existence of the notion of race, as well as the possibility of collecting racial categories, but still mentions it in its antiracist pieces of legislation, only to punish racist acts. As Calvès (2000: 75) notes, "the only race it [French law] knows is the race of the racist." But nowhere in the law is the word race defined or explained. Second, in this admission that racism is present and needs to be fought against, the law admits that discrimination based on race takes place and needs to be addressed through specific policies. This sort of willful ignorance, which Mueller (2020) calls a "commitment to ignorance," and Calvès (2005) terms a "fiction of legal ignorance" or "principle of intentional blindness," serves to prevent any real progress toward racial equity and diversity in French society while also acting to support the dominant logic of colorblind racism.

What is problematic is that through this desire to avoid, at all costs, the acknowledgment and use of racial categories, and the desire to present itself as neutral and raceless, and thus to avoid what is perceived as ethnic pluralism (commonly associated with the United States), France insists on employing a colorblind lens. The result is that some population categories, such as immigrants and foreigners, are lumped together, as if they are the only people of color in France, and therefore denies the existence of French racial minorities. Indeed, per the census categories, it looks as though only people outside the mainstream or majority population can be classed as people of color. This also implies that the official political discourse, based on the available census data, focuses on the "problem of immigrant integration" (Bleich, 2000: 52), which dictates the discourse and the policies. It follows that all policies addressing discrimination are really "integration policies," as if the conversation was solely about integrating immigrants rather than addressing racial inequalities among French citizens. It also implicitly places the burden of integration – the will to succeed at integrating – on the shoulders of immigrants, as if they are the problem and thus carry the responsibility for the discrimination they face and for taking the necessary actions to resolve it. The implication of this ideology is that the divide isn't race but rather citizenship, and that once immigrants are integrated and citizens of France, the issues of discrimination and segregation will disappear, which would prove that racism in this sense doesn't really exist in France and that race is not a salient indicator of inequalities. The fantasy here corresponds to what Bleich (2000) has claimed, namely that France tries to fight racism without acknowledging the existence of races. However, as Bleich (2000) argues, the state may officially ignore races, but the larger public has little hesitation in identifying others according to their perceived physical attributes (skin color among them). In other words, the French state may pretend that races don't exist, but people who live and work in France are at the very least race-conscious.

4

Counting Racial Diversity:
Naming and Numbering

Through an examination of the current census structure in France, this chapter argues that the so-called colorblindness of the French census can be analyzed as a form of colorblind racism that reproduces and maintains racial inequality in France. This chapter critically reviews the existing scholarship on the categorization of race in the census and offers an alternative to previous explanations for the absence of racial statistics in the French census. Using the lens of Bonilla-Silva's (2006) framework on colorblind racism and Feagin's concept of the White racial frame (2009, 2012), the chapter examines the relationship between France's colorblind discourse and the material conditions of racial inequality. The chapter shows that France's universalist and republican ideals, as well as the national identity principle, constructed in opposition to multiculturalism and differentialism, serve as the dominant White racial frames, as conceptualized by Feagin (2009, 2012), that deny the reality of social relations based on race and support colorblind racism while justifying a racialized definition of French nationality.

The question of whether the French census should include racial and ethnic statistics is part of a debate in France that has been going since the start of the 21st century (Simon, 2008a).

IAs well as the collection of racial or ethnic categories in the census being prohibited, it is also illegal in principle for any French government structures, and public or private institutions, to request and hold information that includes racial or ethnic categories. This arguably makes France a colorblind society by law in terms of racial categories.

At the same time, there have been several attempts over the years – mostly unsuccessful – by scholars, nongovernmental organizations, and elected officials to argue for the inclusion of "ethnic statistics," as they have come to be called in France. The most recent attempt was made by a group of local elected officials from different minority groups who advocate for a change in the law. However, a 2010 report written by the Comité pour la Mesure et l'Évaluation de la Diversité et des Discriminations (Comedd, or Committee for the Measure and Evaluation of Diversity and Discriminations) claims that no such law is needed as France already has the necessary statistical tools to measure the diversity of the French population.

This chapter will first review the existing census methods of data collection, as well as its contradicting elements. It will then examine the various strategies, repertoires, and codes that comprise the grammar of colorblindness with regard to census data collection before offering a comparison with other European countries' census methodologies.

Collecting data: methods and contradictions
Overview

A close look at demographic data from INSEE reveals information about sex, age, nationality, country of origin, immigration status, matrimonial status, professional status, residence, and so on, which the law authorizes, but no data on racial or ethnic categories, as otherwise seen in the US census.

The French government does not legally acknowledge race or ethnicity as a social identity marker. Officially, "race" and racial categories do not exist in the census, on the job market, or in the school system. So not only does the census not count race but other public and private institutions are also not allowed to collect information about someone's race or ethnicity for the purpose of classifying them. This also means that those institutions (INSEE, INED, and the CNIL) do not have a working definition of race or ethnicity.

A closer look at the websites of the organizations mentioned in the previous paragraph reveals a remarkable absence of definitions for race or ethnicity. The closest these websites come to mentioning ethnic origins is when they use the national origin of immigrants, foreigners, the acquisition of nationality, or something about the former colonies.

Olivier Monso and Thibaut de Saint Pol (2007) explain that the point of the census is to provide a picture of the different characteristics of the population and that looking at national origins wasn't originally a priority. It was added gradually, connected to the migration flows and changes in French nationality law (Monso and de Saint Pol, 2007). The conceptualization of the foreigner, with regard to the idea of nationality, emerged relatively recently (Weil, 2002). The first law on "nationality" appeared in the Napoleonic Civil Code, although the concept itself only appeared later in the 19th century. Thus the term "nationality" coincides with the implementation of the first real census of the French population. By the late 19th century, there was a shift from the concept of the foreigner to the idea of the "immigrant." Then came the debate over the issue of how to deal with "naturalized French" individuals. Since 1851, the census has classified people into three categories in terms of nationality, distinguishing French by birth, French by acquisition, and foreigners (Simon, 2003).

Not only are racial or ethnic categories and the concept of minority absent from the French census but they are seldom used in social science studies. In France, CNIL defines the legal frame for all surveys that include so-called sensible questions (that is, questions about religion, organization membership, or health condition and sexual preferences). French law authorizes data collection based on nationality or the birthplace of an individual and their parents, but it forbids collecting data on their "real or presumed" racial or ethnic origin. This idea is based on 18th-century values from the French Revolution with the emergence of a new republican citizenship; when France became a republic, its social actors all became citizens of the Republic. Citizenship was then based on the universal revolutionary principles of "liberty, equality, fraternity.

However, as seen in Chapter 1, the word race has been in use in France since as early as the 15th century, and the construction of race-thinking and race-consciousness in and from France, notably with its attention to skin color, can be traced back to the 17th century.

The 18th century witnessed the appearance of the *Livret d'ouvrier* (or Labor booklet), which was an official personal document in the form of a booklet serving as a means to control the working hours and movements of workers, who had to carry the *Livret* with them at all times stating when and where they worked. A worker without their *Livret* was considered a vagabond and could be arrested and punished as such. The *Livret* was more than data collection; it was a means of exerting social control over the workers. The *Livret* made its first appearance in 1781 but was abolished during the French Revolution, only to be reintroduced by Napoleon in 1803 and finally abandoned in 1890.

In 1873, French historian-geographer Louis Dussieux published a book on geography containing political, historical, and other socioeconomic data, as well as ethnographic information. As part of the population description of France, he enumerated five races:

- The Gallo-Roman race (including French and Normans);
- the Celtic race (the Lower-Britons);
- the Iberian race (including Basques, Gascons, Languedoc peoples, Provençal peoples, Ligure peoples, Corsicans, Roussillon peoples);
- the Germanic race (including Germans and Flemish); and
- the Semitic race (Jews).

Additionally, as noted by Monso and de Saint Pol (2007), during the Vichy regime (1940–4), the Germans ordered a census of Jews in the "northern zone," the part of France under direct Nazi occupation. At that point, there were two criteria that defined a person as Jewish: (1) the number of their Jewish grandparents, and (2) their religion. The statutes actually referred to the "Jewish race," though as Monso and de Saint Pol note, this was not imposed by the Nazis but implemented by the Vichy government itself. These statutes were motivated by anti-Semitic policies. According to Weil (2002), the occupation marks an important moment in the "ethnic crises of French nationality." Another significant moment in the history of the French census is the way that censuses were carried out in the French colonies enabled statisticians in Algeria to divide "French persons by birth" into two categories, "Muslims of Algerian origin" and "Other than Muslims of Algerian origin." In other words, they distinguished between whether the person was a "Muslim French person" or not (Kateb, 2004). Furthermore, as Angéline Escafré-Dublet et al (2020) explain, starting in 1946, all inhabitants of French colonies were made citizens of the French Union, including Algerians. This new status implied that citizens of the French Union were now free to travel, particularly to metropolitan France. At that point, a large number of newly naturalized French-Algerians migrated to France. In order to control this new migrant flow and accurately count the number of Algerians in France, the French state scheduled several censuses. The issue, however, was that at least in appearances, the French administration couldn't ask different questions to the colonial migrants and to the metropolitan French citizens, and certainly could not directly ask its metropolitan French citizens whether they were French Muslims from Algeria. Therefore, the French administration asked their census agents to create a distinction between French Muslims of Algeria and other French citizens once the census taking was completed. The 1954 census form asked the following questions:

- Last name and first name;
- date of birth;
- sex;
- place of birth;
- nationality (French by birth, French by naturalization, foreigner/ specify nationality);
- current address;
- years at current address; and
- previous city of residence.

Since the questions did not include specifics about religion or ethnicity, the identification was operated by the census agents when the census forms were processed for coding. For example, for French citizens the first digit was 0, and for French born in metropolitan France the second digit was also 0. On the other hand, census agents were instructed to code 01 when an individual met three criteria: (1) place of birth is Algeria; (2) person reports French nationality; (3) person has an Arab- or Berber-sounding first and last name. A list of the most common Muslim names from the Algerian civil records was provided to the census agents at the time of the coding. Coding was thus left to the agents' interpretation. As an example, a person with a Christian- or Jewish-sounding name was coded as French by birth but as having been born in Algeria. As Escafré-Dublet et al (2020: 4) argue, the issue here is not the use of ethnicity to categorize an individual, but rather identifying that person "ex-post while asserting elsewhere that it is no different from the others." Another problematic issue was that the goal of such identification was not to guarantee equal rights to former colonial subjects but rather to track their presence in metropolitan France.

Contemporary context

It is currently illegal under French law for any questions in the census to include racial categories of any population residing in France.

The 1978 law, "Loi Informatique et Libertés," states that it is forbidden to "collect or treat data with personal characteristics that indicate, directly or indirectly, racial or ethnic origins, political, philosophical, or religious opinions, or union membership of the individuals, or that are related to the health or sexual life of the individuals."

Additionally, in its November 15, 2007 decision, the French Constitutional Council forbids the implementation of research methods to measure social diversity that would contradict the principle of Article 1 of the French Constitution. It accordingly bans 'the treatment of personal data showing directly or indirectly the racial or ethnic origins of the individuals and the introduction of variables such as race or religion in administrative data'. The point of this decision was to declare anti-constitutional an article in an earlier immigration law. Indeed, Article 63 of the law on immigration had proposed modifying the 1978 law by authorizing the collection of ethnic statistics under the control of CNIL in order to measure the diversity of origins of individuals, as well as discrimination and integration. The council had stated that ethnic statistics were contrary to Article 1 of the French Constitution, which assures the equality of all French citizens under the law without any distinction. In addition, the Constitutional Council added that it would be contrary to the Constitution to have an a priori definition of an "ethno-racial frame of reference."

As a result, data on racial or ethnic origins, and the introduction of variables such as race or religion in administrative files, are strictly forbidden. According to Article 226-19 of the Penal Code, the penalty for breaking this law is up to five years in prison and a 300,000 euros fine.

The Constitutional Council nevertheless considers that objective data necessary to examine diversity and integration can be collected on family ancestry of individuals: for example, their name, geographic origin, or nationality prior to acquiring French citizenship. Furthermore, the Constitutional Council also authorizes the collection of surveys examining membership perception: for example, the TeO surveys carried out by INSEE and INED (see Chapter 2) are based on the perception of respondents toward their feeling of group membership.

According to INSEE (2016), the organization itself and other institutes (like INED) produce statistics to measure, among other things, the diversity of French society based on objective data such as birthplace, nationality at birth, and current nationality, which are available in many surveys and population censuses. For INSEE (2016), these objective criteria are largely sufficient to reflect the diversity of the French population and identity and specify possible discrimination or difficulties experienced by certain groups of the population. To go beyond these criteria while still respecting the law (notably the Constitutional Council's 2007 decision), surveys can only use individuals' "feeling of membership," a notion INSEE considers to be less reliable and more subject to contradictory and confusing interpretations than the objective criteria mentioned earlier.

Article 8 of the 1978 "Loi Informatique et Libertés" authorizes some exemptions on a case-by-case basis after evaluation and approval by CNIL. The law says it is possible to collect data about ethnic and racial origins under certain conditions, which are to be examined and approved by CNIL to validate data collection. What is noteworthy is that the law makes use of the words race and ethnicity without ever defining them – they are said but immediately silenced.

However, in contradiction with a seemingly colorblind census, there have been and still are structures in France that seem to acknowledge the notion of race and racial and ethnic categories without describing them as such at an official level.

For example, the Système de Traitement des Infractions Constatées (STIC, or Processing Program of Recorded Offenses) is a police database used to identify the perpetrators and victims of crimes. The database was officially created in 2001 by a decree issued by the Minister of Interior's office but has been in existence since 1985 without any particular legal or ethical oversight.

The information collected about individuals included name, sex, age, height, and other physical attributes. It also included information about 12 "types," which refer to race or ethnicity without officially using those terms (see Table 4.1).

Table 4.1: Racial categories from the STIC police database, 2006

French	English
Blanc (Caucasien)	White (Caucasian)
Méditerranéen	Mediterranean
Gitan	Gypsy
Moyen-Oriental	Middle Eastern
Nord Africain/Maghrébin	North African/Maghrebi
Asiatique/Eurasien	Asian/Eurasian
Amérindien	Amerindian
Indien	Indian
Métis/Mulâtre	Mixed race/Mulatto
Noir	Black
Polynésien	Polynesian
Mélanésien/Canaque	Melanesian/Kanak

Source: Bauer report (2006)

Table 4.2: Racial categories from the STIC database, 2006

French	English
Type européen (Nordique, Caucasien, Méditerranéen)	European type
Type africain/antillais	African/West Indian type
Type métis	Mixed-race type
Type maghrébin	Maghrebi type
Type moyen-oriental	Middle Eastern type
Type asiatique	Asian type
Type indo-pakistanais	Indo-Pakistani type
Type latino-américain	Latino-American type
Type polynésien	Polynesian type
Type mélanésien (dont Canaque)	Melanesian type (of which Kanak)

Source: Bauer report (2006)

In 2006, STIC decided to adopt a new classification system with ten "types" of individuals (see Table 4.2).

By 2009, the STIC database contained detailed information on 5.5 million individuals suspected of committing a criminal offense and more than 28 million victims. In 2011, the STIC database merged with the Judex database system (système Judiciaire de Documentation et d'Exploitation), another database used by the French Gendarmerie (one of the French police forces) that compiles information on criminals who have been arrested by the Gendarmerie. The new database resulting from this merger is called Traitement d'Antécédents Judiciaires (TAJ, or Processing Program of Criminal Background) and is used for inquests. Among other statistics, the information collected for the TAJ includes identity, nationality, birthplace, and direct line of descent, which does not include any explicit reference to race or ethnicity but does not exclude it either.

The STIC had been criticized by CNIL, and such database systems are controversial in France but only in relation to the question of individuals' privacy rights, not specifically because of the collection of racial and ethnic data.

At the corporate level, companies use ethnic or racial statistics as a marketing tool when targeting a specific population of customers. For example, in their 2009 report French NGO SOS Racisme claims (Thomas, 2009) that several public or private entities in France used ethnic or racial statistics to discriminate against minorities. The report cites several case studies of various industries that show the widespread use of ethnic statistics with regard to their customers, clients, or employees to establish quotas against minorities. French demographer François Héran (2005) says that identifying customers or clients with a profiling method is not necessarily statistical information because such a policy does not measure anything, so it is not seen as problematic. At the same time, a 1998 report published by the HCI explicitly recognizes that most forms of discrimination affect "French people of color, notably from overseas French territories or of non-European foreign origin." Fassin (2002) explains that this recognizes that the basis for those inequalities is racial in nature and therefore that races are socially relevant and significant.

France's blind spot: the grammar of colorblindness

White racial frames and colorblind approaches allow racism to flourish and be reproduced.

As seen in this chapter and previous chapters, there seems to be a contradiction between discourse and practice. On the one hand, it is illegal to use racial or ethnic categories in the French census on the grounds that doing so would reinforce the stigmatization of minorities and lead to an increase in racism. But on the other hand, racial categories are already in use by different institutions and structures, however unofficial and controversial, and most French social scientists outside of INSEE seem to agree that measuring racial or ethnic membership has become a necessity. This led Simon (2008a) to claim that the French colorblind approach to not looking at differences (and analyzing them) is in fact a "choice of ignorance" in that it ignores the experiences of prejudice and discrimination that these "invisible" categories experience every day.

Social scientists ask the question: "What is at the heart of this contradiction, and what are the implications of such avoidance?"

The following part of the chapter begins with a review of current explanations by French scholars of the absence of racial statistics. The chapter will then offer an alternative to such explanations. In particular, the chapter argues that the so-called colorblindness of the French census can be analyzed as a form of colorblind racism using the lens of Bonilla-Silva's (2006) framework. Indeed, this chapter shows that in the debate over ethnic statistics in France, ideas about universalism, national identity, and republican ideals, constructed as the rampart against differentialism, serve as the dominant White racial frames (as conceptualized by Feagin 2009, 2012) that deny the reality of social relations based on race while justifying a racialized definition of French national identity.

The racialist frame: the specter of France's past

A theoretical argument has been made by several scholars that the use of race and racial categories – and the essentialist concept of race – has historically served to create hierarchies between groups and promote systems of oppression. Indeed, for some scholars, the avoidance of racial statistics reflects a malaise vis-à-vis the history of French immigration because these "visible minorities," as they're often called in the media, carry the weight of a history marked with colonization and oppression. As Louis-Georges Tin (2008) says, there is a "name taboo" and a "number taboo." For example, as exemplified by the identification data collected about Jews and Communists in France by the French police helping the Gestapo deport thousands of people to extermination camps, the relationship France has with "fichier" and "fichage" (government databases) is more complicated than previously thought.

Indeed, Pap Ndiaye (2006) explains that it has now been established that the modern notion of race was created to justify colonial domination in general, and slavery in particular. Therefore, any reflection about skin color is inevitably linked to an acknowledgment of the relationship between domination and means of production. And so, on the one hand, by not using race or racial categories, the underlying assumption is that racism will be avoided (Fassin, 2006). On the other hand, the fear is that if essentialist categories are produced and used (based on real or constructed biological differences), difference and otherness become essentialized, which in turn justifies a political order that already does so, and essentialized populations are therefore officially stigmatized. Héran (2005) similarly argues that France has a long history of legal discrimination against Black and Asian minorities, where classification methods were used against them. Because it has been done before with the impunity of the state, there is a real concern that similar types of statistics could be misused. According to Fassin (2006), the social sciences have given reasons to be concerned about the use of such terminology. For example, *The Bell Curve* (Herrnstein and Murray, 1994) established a supposed scientific connection between social inequalities and race, "proving" that if Black people are at the bottom of the social ladder it is because lower intelligence is engrained in their genes (hence supposedly linking someone's IQ to their genes). Linking biology and race is a form of "racialism," or even racism, which could further help justify the repeal of welfare or affirmative action policies (Fassin, 2006). As a result, there is a real fear of seeing eugenics or social Darwinism reemerge in France if the government were to allow the collection of racial statistics. Additionally, Simon and Stavo-Debauge (2004) talk about a controversy that divided demographers in France in 1999: as seen in previous chapters, this is when a generic defiance toward ethnic statistics emerged after a debate on the content of statistics regarding the status of immigrants in the census. The controversy opposed the believers in the status quo in terms of categories and the challengers who wanted to introduce new categories that went beyond the nationality criteria. This controversy has been presented as an opposition between the "ethnicists" and the "republicans" (defenders of the universal ideals of the French Republic). From then on, the latter camp has argued that including racial or ethnic categories would ethnicize France further in how individuals experience their social relations and identities, that is, it would make ethnic identity a central feature of French society and social status and identity. The controversy was particularly acrimonious because the stakes go beyond the simple scientific or technical aspect of the question. It is not just an issue of an analytical concept or principles but about transforming the way experts and individuals construct knowledge about their world and how they represent it. This demographic debate shows how problematic it is to talk and think about the concept of race in France, let alone address issues of racism and discrimination. Finally, groups like SOS Racisme are opposed to the use of ethnic statistics: they launched a call on October 26, 2007 saying that they "oppose a State that is trying to rehabilitate a racial nomenclature based on skin color or that is trying to establish an ethnic-religious reference on the basis of origins or religious membership." For them, ethnic statistics would mark the return of a "colonial France or the one from before August 1944" and would only serve to support "racial stereotypes." In a similar vein, statistician Stéphane Jugnot (2007) argues that the American approach to counting races conveys a "racial, or even racist, vision of humanity" and that discrimination comes from "the eye of the beholder who sees the other as a Black, as a 'dark-skinned' person." Jugnot claims that classifying people into racial categories will give legitimacy (or justify) those who wants to rank racial minorities with racist terms. Yet, as noted by Fassin (2006), racial categories have been used by scholars in their research and teachings; for example, sickle-cell disease, or drépanocytose, is sometimes described as a disease of "the blacks"; Tay–Sachs disease as a "disease of the Jews"; and cystic fibrosis, the mucoviscidose of the Caucasians. Additionally, in 2007, the Constitutional Council in France validated Article 13 of an immigration law introducing DNA testing regarding legal rights for foreigners (where foreigners who can prove, with DNA testing, kinship to family residing in France, may claim legal rights for residency in France), but at the same time it rejected Article 63, which would have allowed for the collection of ethnic statistics. DNA testing is supposed to help prospective migrants prove their links to relatives living in France. This bill was judged highly controversial by many human rights groups in France, who argue that the law is reminiscent of French policies under Nazi occupation that discriminated against Jews by virtue of their biological heritage. However, the Constitutional Council made it clear that ethnic statistics were a "yellow line" that could not be crossed. Here resides the true paradox of the colorblind French census. On the one hand, social actors are creating their own categories that include race and/or ethnicity and "believe in their existence" while also formulating stereotypes and prejudices based on those constructed and perceived racial or ethnic categories, which may in turn lead to discrimination. On the other hand, there is still no working legal or administrative definition of the word or category of race in France. However, for Simon (2003), through the use of euphemisms (the "national origin" question), the French census already acknowledges the existence of presupposed racial or ethnic characteristics. Race and nationality are of course not interchangeable, but because the census does not allow for the recognition of racial categories, Hargreaves (2007: 11) argues that racial minorities with French nationality are "in statistical terms lost almost without trace."

The universalist frame

The debate over racial statistics has been framed by some French scholars and politicians as a supposed opposition between a French republican universalism on the one hand and a differentialist communitarianism on the other. The universalism of the French Republic goes back to the ideal that, after the 1789 French Revolution from which the Republic of France emerged, all subjects would become French citizens with equal rights under a single political system. The invisibility of difference was supposed to imply equality in status and rights. This constructed ideal is opposed to a pluralistic France with diverse identities that would divide the nation into separate communities. However, the notion of a "French universalism" that is so often used in political speeches and media articles is an inherent contradiction in terms: it implies that there exist values that are both universal and that apply specifically to the French context, and all other values, norms, and practices are to be evaluated against this model that is both universal and specifically French. Additionally, using Bonilla-Silva's concept of colorblind racism (2006), it can be argued that the universalist ideal presented in defense of a presumed colorblind census is a veil hiding racial realities and preventing the examination of racial inequalities in France. As such, the refusal to account for race in the French census can be analyzed as a form of colorblind racism that helps maintain the status quo. According to Bonilla-Silva (2006: 2), White people have developed powerful explanations that have ultimately become justifications for contemporary racial inequality. These explanations emanate from a new racial ideology that he calls colorblind racism. Colorblind racism rests on several master frames. In the case of the French census, the central frames justifying the status quo are the universalist ideal and the question of national identity, which can be explained using Feagin's concept of the White racial frame (2009, 2012). According to Feagin, White racial frames are created to maintain and rationalize White privilege and power. The White racial frame has been perpetuated by the White elite, it is dominant, and has provided the main vantage point for many years from which most White people have viewed and interpreted society. Universalism is that vantage point. As Castel (2007) proclaims, this idealized universalism has become blind to diversity and has in fact led to a stigmatization of ethnic differences, where those stigmatized by the labels feel trapped in an ascribed and denigrated identity. It is a contradiction in terms: on the one hand, there is resistance to using the concept of race because it overly emphasizes the differences in opposition to a single unified national identity. Thinking in terms of races would thus be against the whole model of integration *à la française*, which implies universalism without plurality. Yet, on the other hand, through racial profiling, discrimination, and bigoted attitudes, French people of color are reminded every day that they are in fact different and that they have a different skin (and also perhaps different accents and customs and foods) and that they'll never be considered the same as the "real" French because of these differences, regardless of having been born in France. Using Feagin's White racial frame, the underlying assumption of universalism is that to be truly French one has to be White. Therefore, universalism is not as colorblind as its defenders claim. The paradox created by a colorblind census lies in the disconnect between the official rhetoric on racial categories and the less official practices of racial enumeration and the social realities: by denying the existence of racial categories and race's social significance, it also denies the existence of racial minorities in France and their precarious social standing, as a result of which they face discrimination and segregation. So when racial minority organizations claim Blackness, White people think they are threatening the republican order (Fassin, 2006). This is what Feagin (2009, 2012) would call the power of White racial hegemony: in line with the idea of White racial framing, the White racial hegemony perspective argues that systemic racism has evolved and, rather than operating in an overt way, it has become pervasive by "exercising control over cultural beliefs and ideologies, as well as the key legitimizing institutions of society through which they are expressed" (Neubeck and Cazenave, 2001: 22). It is hegemonic in its ideological form and effect so that it ensures White power and privilege. It imposes its "ideological code," using Dorothy Smith's terminology (1993), onto all interpretations of race and racism. It is this ideological hegemony that allows the rationalization and justification of a seemingly colorblind census. In 2005, French philosophers Pierre-André Taguieff and Alain Finkielkraut signed a petition against what they call an "anti-Whites racism," denouncing the shift of French society toward multiculturalism and communitarianism. Denouncing antiWhite aggression, Taguieff and Finkielkraut said that "we talked about David, we talked about Kader, but who talks about Sébastien?" The names used by the petitioners are supposed to "sound" Jewish, Arab, and French, their claim being that the aggressions happened because the victims were French, but that the press doesn't mention them because they are French. These aggressions, petitioners claimed, prove that there exists a form of "Francophobia." The call was heavily criticized by antiracist associations and intellectuals. But what's remarkable is that the petitioners were denouncing something while at the same time acknowledging its existence: they railed against communitarianism and the use of "race" to define identities while simultaneously naming the races. They used the term "French" to mean "Whites" and vice versa, and by silent opposition, also named the "Other," through the use of "ratonnades" ("ratons" is a derogatory French term referring to people from North Africa, whereas "ratonnades" are acts of racist violence committed against North Africans or individuals of North African descent). In other words, says Esther Benbassa (2005), it is a "claim of whiteness." At the same time, this is a hidden acknowledgment of a very French multiculturalism, since the first names used in the petition do refer to an idea of a Jewish, Arab and White France by the petitioners' standards. Finkielkraut's affirmation that there is a "Francophobia" akin to the existence of an Islamophobia is basically a double acknowledgment: on the one hand, it implies that different racial groups exist and can experience racism; and on the other hand, calling "anti-White racism" "Francophobia" creates the implication that French equals White and White equals French. And so, the proponents of the argument against racial statistics in the name of a struggle against communitarianism are also in fact claiming the existence of races and the existence of a superior race since, in this case, only White people in France are French.

The national identity frame

In 2007, then presidential candidate Nicolas Sarkozy proposed the creation of a "ministère de l'immigration et de l'identité nationale" (a minister of immigration and national identity), a post he subsequently created once in office. The announcement provoked an outcry in the political and academic arenas, although Jean-Marie Le Pen, the then leader of the extreme right party Front National (or National Front), approved the idea while criticizing Sarkozy for hunting on his turf. Underlined by the creation of the new ministerial post was the question of nationality and national identity: What does it mean to be French? Historian Gerard Noiriel (2007a) explains that the construction of the idea of a national identity in France emerged in the Third Republic. School plays a major role in this: children all read the same textbooks and are subjected to the same homogenized culture promoted by the republican state. The press also plays an important role in the construction of a system of common references in that, beginning in the 1870s, many people started reading the same press. The national press conveys frames of reference that are the same for everyone. The problem with associating words like national identity and immigration is that not only does it imply an antagonistic relation between the two terms but it also establishes a direct connection between them. Indeed, the very fact that it creates an association of ideas in people's minds is problematic because it implies an opposition and a threat, which is the same rhetoric that has been used by the National Front since the 1980s with the association of immigration and national identity as its central anti-immigration theme (Noiriel, 2007a).

Two years later, in the fall of 2009, Eric Besson (the then Minister of Immigration, Integration, and National Identity) announced that the French government would launch a public debate about national identity. Participants were to include NGOs, unions, teachers, parents, students, and local officials, with a presentation of conclusions to take place at the end of February 2010, a few months before regional elections. Some 200 questions revolved around around the twin themes of what it means to be French today and "the contribution of immigration to national identity?" The themes to be addressed dealt with a definition of "our nation," the idea of national solidarity, secularism (French "laïcité"), the culinary arts, churches' steeples (as opposed to minarets), and the idea of making young people sing the national anthem, the Marseillaise, at least once a year.

Several French scholars (including Michel Wievorka and Vincent Tiberj) argued that the problem with launching such a debate in those terms was that it automatically focused and opposed national identity and immigrants. And by introducing the debate in the form of a governmental questionnaire, it strengthened the negative association between national identity and immigration, legitimizing the rhetoric of the extreme right in France, as this was now being used by the mainstream right. French social scientists did not see the debate as an open and honest conversation but rather as a way to crystallize the opposition between national identity and immigration. The national identity debate was also a way for the government to denounce a supposedly emerging communitarianism that works against the French republican ideal of national identity. Other, more specific questions included: "Is our republic multicultural?," "Are the values of a national identity compatible with communitarianism?," and "Should the Republic go further in its fight against communitarianism?" Hence the problem was not the debate on national identity per se but that the French government framed it in opposing terms, so that the debate was in fact skewed because a White racial frame was used to define French national identity, creating a negative connotation about what might be "different."

According to Feagin (2009, 2012), the White racial frame relies, among other things, on racialized emotions and racial narratives and interpretations widely accepted among White people that justify a particular racial order beneficial to White people. Thus the definition of "Frenchness" and of the "Other" is based on the assumption that French nationality means being White, while those who are not White are by default non-French. But all of this was done under the premise of colorblindness: using Bonilla-Silva's perspective (2006: 3), "the ideology of colorblindness seems like 'racism lite,'" because the narratives and practices are apparently nonracial. This national identity debate is an illustration of the problematic nature of a colorblind census that asks for the nationality of individuals, as the question is ultimately about naming. For example, in 2009 Dominique Lefebvre, the Mayor of Cergy (a suburb of Paris), declared that 45 percent of his team was composed of elected officials from "visible minorities who are having a hard time being recognized as full citizens." He added that some members of his team were having a hard time feeling French, like "young French people from immigration." This is essentially the core of the problem: recognizing that minorities are "visible," presumably on the basis of their skin color, while the census and other institutions are supposed to be colorblind and not "see" race; but it is also a recognition of those minorities' unequal treatment, all the while emphasizing their difference and as such treating them as inferior, since they are not the "real" French. At about the same time that this debate was taking place, another event was also happening, the election of Miss France 2010. A few days before the final round of voting, the organization's founder, Geneviève de Fontenay, declared that she dreamed of "seeing a 'beurette' girl become Miss France" (a colloquial term for "North African"; reversed syllables of the word "Arabe" in French or Arabic, with a feminine ending to it). The title of Miss France 2010 was ultimately won by Ms. Malika Ménard. In one of the interviews following her victory, and picking up on De Fontenay's comment, she was asked whether she was of a mixed origin, to which she answered that she was "100 percent French," adding that her name didn't have any origin, that it was a "symbol of tolerance" of her parents, and also that her mother and grandmother had lived in Morocco. The media didn't really follow-up on this brief comment, although the timing in itself was interesting. So there it was again: a first name that sounded strange or different was assumed not to be French, to be of another race (without saying it), while at the same time confirming that if a name has "no origin," then it must be French and thus White. Also, by affirming that she was "100 percent French," Ménard meant that her blood was 100 percent French because it did not have any foreign element – if it did, then it would be foreign, not French, and no one would know what to call it. There is a hidden acknowledgment here of a connection between race and blood (100 percent French versus not 100 percent) comparable to the idea of blood quantum as used by Native Americans, or the concept of the one-drop rule used for Black people in the United States. The notion of blood quantum for Native Americans refers to blood quantum laws in the United States, which legally defined individuals' membership to a Native American tribe according to their blood quantum – the fraction of a person's ancestors documented as full-blood Native Americans. The notion of the one-drop rule was a legal system for the racial classification and assignation of Blacks in the United States. It stated that a person with one Black ancestor in their family was automatically considered black.

As Fassin (2006) notes, when mentioning racial minorities, the French connect the idea of being a racial minority with not being French and thus with being an immigrant (hence the expressions "second generation" and "of immigrant descent"). Someone's French nationality will always be questioned on the basis of their skin color (despite a colorblind census stating their nationality as "French"). Fassin (2006) says that the confusion that currently exists between the categories "foreigner" and "immigrant," or between "foreigner" and "of foreign origin," and between "racial" and "ethnic," does not result from a mistake or an error over how to define those categories correctly. For example, Fassin (2006) argues, it would not help as some have suggested to replace the detestable expression "of French stock" (referring to the supposed purity of French blood) with the expression "French person of France," which is highly problematic as well. This reflects a degree of discomfort, to say the least, with admitting that the effective nationality of a person matters less than their perceived otherness and that there are people in France who despite being French continue to be perceived as "not from around here."

This chapter argues that such assumptions are an illustration of colorblind racism. Indeed, as Bonilla-Silva (2006) shows, colorblind ideology helps White people deny any awareness of racial differences as long as the word "race" isn't pronounced. But there is a suspicion that an individual cannot truly be French if they are not White. That person will forever be seen as an immigrant and will never be legitimate and legitimized, regardless of identification proving their French nationality. This "discomfort" in naming reveals a "profound and unacceptable truth" (Fassin, 2006), namely that "the actual nationality matters far less than the perceived otherness." As Castel (2007) argues, it is as if minorities will always have a "deficient habitus." Etienne Balibar (2007) adds to this the idea that the category of "minorities" is forever connected with "the social category of the hereditary condition of immigrant." Racial minorities are thus viewed as the "foreigners from within" regardless of having acquired French nationality. It is basically an accumulation of handicaps (Balibar, 2007).

Comparative case studies in Europe

None of the EU's member states have established an absolute prohibition on the collection of racial and ethnic data, but they do not make it mandatory either, with the exception of Finland, Ireland, and the United Kingdom (Farkas, 2017).

According to Lilla Farkas (2017), all three of the latter countries require racial or ethnic data collection as part of their equality planning. In Finland, all government institutions, as well as all employers, must assess their equality levels. In Ireland, the Irish Human Rights and Equality Commission Act 2014 (Article 42) mandates all Irish state-funded institutions to address the issue of discrimination while promoting equality and the protection of human rights in relation to discrimination. This mandate requires that state institutions provide an annual report that includes racial or ethnic data. Under the UK's Equality Act 2010, public authorities must collect data in order to monitor progress made on the promotion of equal opportunity. Simon (2017) explains that ethnic statistics have been collected in the UK's census since 1991, as part of its equality policies.

Racial and ethnic data collection is also promoted in other European countries, albeit not as comprehensively. For example, in the Netherlands, cities that fall under the 2009 Municipal Antidiscrimination Facilities Act must provide a registration system that allows for complaints about discrimination. In 2007, the Ministry of Safety and Justice issued the Dutch Discrimination Instruction specifically for the police, public prosecutors, and other administrations such as the Antidiscrimination Bureau. The instruction provides guidelines on collecting data in a consistent way for the prosecution of discrimination cases to be effective (Farkas, 2017). In other countries, like Romania and Hungary, the EU requires authorities to collect data on the ethnicity of the beneficiaries (based on voluntary declarations) of projects financed by European funds. In Sweden, "ethnic origin" is the term that is more commonly used in public administrative documents. In Belgium, the Interfederal Centre for Equal Opportunities publishes a biannual Diversity Barometer to examine attitudes toward minorities as well as the participation level of ethnic and racial minorities in employment, education, and so forth (Farkas, 2017).

Simon (2017) shows that out of 46 countries in the Council of Europe, 22 do ask questions about ethnicity or a related category (such as nationality, here understood as ethnic affiliation), and in most of those cases, ethnicity refers to national minorities rather than immigrants.

Additionally, Beaman (2019) explains that from the standpoint of perception and framing, Whiteness is the default category in the UK, where British equals being White. In a similar way, Beaman (2019) shows that in Germany, race and ethnicity are used to distinguish who is and who is not German, and the assumption is that a nonWhite individual is suspected of not being German. Another example is the Netherlands, which uses terms like "autochthon" (from this soil) and "allochthon" (from another soil) as racial labels to differentiate Dutch and non-Dutch.

Conclusion

According to Héran (2005), there is no need to create new categories when the French census already has operating classifications. Indeed, says Héran, the French system uses a straightforward and simple category to describe immigrants and French of immigrant descent in terms of their birthplace and national origins. From Héran's perspective, it is similar to the "foreign-born" category of the American census. However, it seems that this detailed categorization of national origins only focuses on immigrants and second-generation immigrants or French of immigrant descent. As a matter of fact, when the French press refers to minorities living in the suburbs, they often use the terms "French of immigrant descent" (even though these may be France-born citizens) as euphemisms for "ethnic minorities." Héran (2005) argues that there is a misconception about the French census and the question of ethnic statistics. He says that it is in fact possible to differentiate French individuals in terms of their origins and describe the origins of immigrants and their children who have acquired French nationality. In other words, it is possible to know if people are French by birth or by acquisition of citizenship. This has been in place since 1871. Thus the French census is perfectly capable, Héran (2005) argues, of estimating the number of "Polish, Italians, Spanish, Portuguese, Algerians, Turks, Vietnamese, etc" who have acquired French nationality. In 2006, INED proposed measuring the social integration of second generations of Turks and Moroccans. The idea was authorized by CNIL, but it did not receive everyone's support. For example, the leaders of the Mouvement contre le Racisme et pour l'Amitié entre les Peuples (MRAP, or Movement Against Racism and for Friendship between Peoples), the Ligue des Droits de l'Homme (LDH, or Human Rights League), and SOS Racisme, three major French human and civil rights organizations, said that including race and ethnicity in census statistics was dangerous and unnecessary. They argued that including racial or ethnic categories was not "a necessity to fight against discrimination" and instead claimed that it would legitimize the notion of "race," which has no scientific basis. Similarly, in 2007, under the initiative of Professor Jean-François Amadieu (director of the Observatoire des Discriminations), about 30 researchers, union leaders, and other association leaders published a petition claiming that ethnic statistics were useless and dangerous. They explained that the introduction in France of an ethno-racial reference and identifying the population according to such criteria would legitimize the notion of race, which has no biological character. Fassin (2006) argues that racial minorities in France do not wish to focus on race (and their racial identity) because they wish to assimilate and for their racial identity to disappear, with the thought that they will become more accepted (within and by the White population) if they don't focus on their own racial identity. Héran (2005), meanwhile, has responded to the criticisms of colorblindness by saying that it is not that the French census is blind or in denial or avoiding consciously recognizing race but that it is an "active opposition to take the 'visible' into consideration when it is about the fate of individuals." Of course, Héran admits, everyone can perceive and see personal signs or symbols of difference (language, accent, last name, clothing, physical appearance) that may connect to a foreign origin, but in France, Héran says, there is an understanding that although visible in the public space, those differences should not be taken into consideration legally or practically when it comes to job or university applications. From his perspective, the so-called colorblindness of the French census is in fact an effort to neutralize the differences by dismissing them despite their visibility. The whole idea behind this is to say that the French system is able to differentiate but does not discriminate. However, using Bonilla-Silva's concept of colorblind racism and Feagin's White racial framing perspective, this chapter has offered an alternative to previous analyses. Indeed, this chapter has demonstrated that the so-called colorblind French census can be analyzed as a type of colorblind racism, with universalism and national identity as the central White racial frames justifying the status quo. As Feagin and Adia Wingfield (2013: 13) argue, this kind of system not only rationalizes a racial order but also creates a "dominant racial hierarchy." Following this claim, the chapter also argued that the republican ideal of universalism in fact leads to significant levels of discrimination against minorities in France, because it pretends races are not relevant and significant demographically or sociologically. So not only does the absence of racial categories prevent the French census from obtaining objective data to observe discrimination and racism but it actually produces racism because it frames a supposedly "real" French national identity as White by the simple virtue that no one can be counted differently. In the French census, if a person isn't White, they simply don't have cognized status. The French census in its colorblindness isn't acknowledging that being French can and does mean an entire array of races and colors and ethnicities. By ignoring differences, it establishes a system where only the dominant group can enjoy the full exercise of political rights. It denies diversity, thus reproducing colorblind racism. The colorblind census thus presents and supports a nation of Whiteness, not colorblindness. Scholars like Weil (2005) and Hargreaves (2007) argue that if race and ethnicity were included in the census and other data collection systems, social scientists would be able to examine the social mobility of racial minorities over time in France and therefore argue for the implementation of appropriate public policies. Hence this refusal to incorporate racial and ethnic data in state-sponsored data collection in France allows the state to hide and maintain the social reality of institutionalized discrimination. The negative effect of this illusory colorblind policy of the French census is that the universalism and nationality principles that imply equality in rights mask an inequality in facts. As Eric Macé (2005) underlines, the problem is that "in France we have an institutional racism that we are not allowed to treat institutionally." The colorblind policy of the French census gives it the appearance of universalism and implies a normality that is "normal" only for the White French.

Here resides the true paradox of the colorblind French census. On the one hand, social actors have created their own categories that include race and/or ethnicity and "believe in their existence," while also formulating stereotypes and prejudices based on those constructed and perceived racial or ethnic categories, which may in turn lead to discrimination. However, for Simon (2003), through the use of euphemisms (the "national origin" question), the French census already acknowledges the existence of presupposed racial or ethnic characteristics. Race and nationality are not interchangeable, but because the census does not allow for the recognition of racial categories, Hargreaves (2007: 11) argues that racial minorities with French nationality are "in statistical terms lost almost without trace."

At the same time, and as also seen in other European models, French nationality is associated with Whiteness, which indicates that, contrary to official policy, French society does not really deny the existence of Whiteness but pretends it is not there while also making it the norm, the hegemony even, which measures membership of French nationality against the others, who are not White.

Martinique-born writer Frantz Fanon wrote (1967) that he could never be seen as French despite having been born in a French "departement" and spending time in metropolitan France. According to Beaman (2019: 7), Fanon's writings show us how, despite the denial and avoidance of racial categories, race is in fact a significant element of social life in France at the micro, meso, and macro levels.

5

Rioting the Residences and Reclaiming the Republic

Graham Murray called them "France's Hurricane Katrina" (2006: 26). French philosopher Alain Badiou wrote in the French newspaper *Le Monde* (November 15, 2005) that "we have the riots we deserve." Social scientists and politicians in France and elsewhere have agreed: France's October–November 2005 riots that started in the suburbs of Paris, the *banlieues*, shook the three pillars of the French republican principles that defined the 1789 French Revolution – "liberty, equality, fraternity."

Ethnic riots have taken place in France for over 20 years, since the riots between police and ethnic minorities in the suburbs of Lyon, France, in 1981 and 1983, and then in 1990, 1991, 1993, and later (Roché, 2006). However, what made the 2005 riots new and unique was their prolonged duration, as well as their persistence for almost three weeks, despite a strong police presence.

What also appears to be new was the strategy used by the government to seemingly maintain tension by using confrontational language on the one hand and a rhetoric of fear and security on the other.

The riots have been defined and categorized by scholars as "ethnic riots" because they involved "episodes of sustained collective violence with an ethnic, racial, religious, or xenophobic character" (Bleich et al, 2010: 271). Previous research on the 2005 French riots has focused primarily on the social and racial inequality, and the resulting social and racial fracture, that exists in the *banlieues* of France for disenfranchised minority groups; this racial inequality has been analyzed as the main explanation for these explosive riots that burned the suburbs of France, and Paris in particular (Hargreaves, 2005; Weil, 2005; Castel, 2007; Fassin and Fassin, 2009). However, despite a considerable amount of scholarship written on the place of the riots in French integration politics, very little attention has been paid to the role of the French government's response in how the riots developed and were represented and dealt with, although a few scholars have acknowledged its significance (Macé, 2005; Murray, 2006; Roché, 2006; Waddington and King, 2012).

Through a review of public speeches, media declarations, and interviews by French government officials and influential intellectuals, this chapter examines the language used and the measures taken by the French government over the course of the events. Using the White racial frame perspective (as articulated by Feagin, 2010b, 2012) and the colorblind framework (as formulated by Bonilla-Silva, 2006), the chapter argues that the government's response to the riots shows that (1) by applying a White racial frame to the riots against the rioters, the state was able to denigrate the rioters and deny any legitimacy to the riots themselves; and that (2) by applying colorblind racist labels to the rioters, the state was able to discredit the revolt in order to rationalize and justify a set of repressive tactics and racist measures without "sounding racist." The chapter reveals that the French government ultimately normalized a racial frame about the riots through colorblind racist rhetoric and practices, indicating the rise of a legitimized racism that is becoming a dominant and widely accepted view in the political arena in France.

This chapter will first describe the 2005 French riots that took place in the French *banlieues*. It will then review the current literature that has examined the riots and provide an analysis of the riots as they pertain to the larger question of racial identity. Finally, it will demonstrate the 2005 riots' significance in the larger context of the discursive and institutional structure that is the French model with regard to race and racism.

Political rhetoric

Language and rhetoric are at the center of this chapter. Political rhetoric is not treated as epiphenomenal to the riots but rather analyzed as a central phenomenon. Peter Berger (1969: 20) claims that individuals use language to impose order on reality, and that therefore the use of language orders the physical reality. Rhetoric in this regard can be defined as symbolic action in which people engage, and when they do, they participate in the construction of social reality and ascribe meanings to that reality. More specifically, this chapter focuses on the rhetoric employed by representatives of the French government and other elected officials over the course of the 2005 riots and how that rhetoric supports the rise of legitimized racism in France. For the purpose of this chapter, rhetoric isn't limited to Aristotle's definition of rhetoric as the "available means of persuasion." Rather, this chapter uses Kevin Michael DeLuca's perspective on rhetoric as "the mobilization of signs for the articulation of identities, ideologies, consciousness, communities, publics, and cultures" (1999: 17). As such, the discourse employed by the French government can be analyzed as a form of domination that "creates and sustains social practices which control the dominated" (DeLuca, 1999: 17).

Through rhetoric, then, a social framing is at work, where ideological frames are imposed on social events and cultural texts. Additionally, in Michel Foucault's perspective (1984), rhetorical procedures can be analyzed as ways of producing events and decisions that imply action. Indeed, as argued by Karlyn Kohrs Campbell, rhetoric is action, and people possess rhetorical agency: "[R]hetorical agency is the capacity to act, that is, to have the competence to speak or write in a way that will be recognized or heeded by others in one's community" (2005: 3). The French government has rhetorical agency, while the rioters lack any such agency. The rioters don't get to participate in the construction of the social reality; in fact, they have no control over what is said about them and about the riots. That is because, according to Roland Barthes (1970), rhetoric can be viewed as social practice and language as power owned by the elite to act in the world, therefore having rhetorical agency. And for Foucault (1984: 110), discourse is "the thing for which and by which there is struggle"; it is "the power which is to be seized." In this sense, rhetoric is an instrument of power as well as "the means by which people engage in a struggle for power" (Palczewski et al, 2012: 23). Finally, the rhetoric used by the French government serves to mobilize symbols to act and justify its actions (policies), therefore asserting its power and hegemony. Indeed, in a Gramscian perspective (Palczewski et al, 2012: 25), hegemony is constructed and maintained by rhetorical actions. Using a Gramscian approach (Zompetti, 1997), hegemonic ideology means that social control is accomplished through the control of ideas. Such hegemony reduces one's agency because it limits the choices that make sense, that give meaning and interpretation.

Chronology of events: how the house burned down

The French ethnic riots of October–November 2005 started in the Paris suburb of Clichy-sous-Bois (zip code 93, in the department of Seine-St-Denis, northeast of Paris), where a high percentage of immigrants and racial minorities reside, particularly North African or sub-Saharan African minorities. Specifically, on the evening of October 27, 2005 in Clichy-sous-Bois, three minors, Bouna Traoré (15 years old), Zyed Benna (17 years old), both from African-Maghrebi families, and Muhittin, or Muttin, Altun (17 years old), from a Turkish family, were chased by the police as they were returning home from a football game. They ran and jumped over the fence of an electric transformer (owned by France's national electric company, Electricité de France or EDF). Two of them, Bouna Traoré and Zyed Benna, were electrocuted and killed; Muttin Altun, seriously burned, ran back toward his projects, where Bouna Traoré's brother found him.2 The word spread fast in the *cité*, and shortly afterward confrontations started between a dozen young men and the police in the area. Overnight, some cars were burned, and then a kindergarten as well as some local stores and bus shelters were damaged. The next day, October 28, Muttin Altun was brought in for police interrogation.

The riots had begun. During the night of October 28, more violent altercations occurred between young men and the police, and the violence reached other nearby *cités*. On October 29, 400 people marched silently in Clichy-sous-Bois wearing white T-shirts that read *Morts pour Rien* (Dead for Nothing), provided by the association Au-delà Des Mots (ADM, or Beyond Words), which was founded in memory of Bouna Traoré and Zyed Benna. Graffiti saying "Bouna, may you rest in peace" could be seen on the buildings along the street.

In a matter of days, the riots expanded to other towns of the 93 zip code. Cars were the primary targets of the attacks, but public property was also damaged. By November 7, about 1,400 cars had burned, and schools and public transportation properties had been destroyed. Rioters and the police clashed on the streets, so much so that on November 9 the government decided to put France under a state of emergency and apply the 1955 state of emergency law to the entire French continental territory. The riots continued, and on November 11, while the government commemorated the First World War Armistice of 1918, about 300 people united in a collection of associations called Banlieues Respect (Suburbs Respect) and began to march for peace in the center of Paris, asking for the violence to stop. Security was reinforced in the area of the march with an additional 2,200 police. At night, the riots still raged. By November 12, riots had spread to other suburbs of Paris and to all the major cities of France (except Marseille). Over the nights of November 12 and 13, the violence continued, although it had decreased and become less prevalent in the Parisian suburbs than in the rest of the country. On November 16, the front page of the French daily newspaper *Libération* stated, "France is burning less and less." By November 17, the riots seemed to be over. Over the course of the riots, 4,770 individuals were arrested for questioning by the police, 763 of whom received prison sentences, of which 118 were minors.3 Additionally, besides these arrests and jail sentences, anywhere between ten and 120 people among the individuals arrested were foreign nationals and were immediately deported back to their country of origin. However, the cabinet of the Minister of Interior never gave an official count of the number of deportations or of the countries of deportation. Five policemen were also indicted under the charge of assaulting a young man beaten up by the police in front of television cameras.

The geography of the riots is a significant and relevant element. As previously mentioned, the city of Clichy-sous-Bois, where the riots started, is a suburb northeast of Paris with a population of almost 30,000 inhabitants located in the department of Seine-St-Denis. According to the 2009 census, the department of Seine-St-Denis has a population of about 1,500,000 divided into 40 communes, one of which is the city of Clichy-sous-Bois. The zip code for the Seine-St-Denis department is 93 and is identified in local slang as "the 9-3" ("the ninety-three" or "the nine-three"), which often implies a reference to *cités* like in Clichy-sous-Bois. From 1930 to 1950, the Seine-St-Denis department was known as the "Red Belt," a residential area for a working-class population, with dominant Communist local governments. Since the 1960s, when the development of housing projects or *cités* increased, the department of Seine-St-Denis has become the French department with the highest proportion of immigrants – 21.7 percent. Furthermore, according to French demographers Bernard Aubry and Michèle Tribalat (2009), the 2005 demographic records show that 57 percent of all minors born in France residing in the department of Seine-St-Denis have at least one parent of foreign origin (77 percent for minors residing in the city of Clichy-sous-Bois). Additionally, Aubry and Tribalat (2009) show that in the Seine-St-Denis department, out of the 57 percent of minors born in France with at least one parent of foreign origin, 22 percent of them have at least one parent from North Africa and 16 percent have at least one parent from sub-Saharan Africa. However, because France does not allow the collection of ethnic (including religious) or racial data for census purposes, these percentages do not include a specific ratio of racial and ethnic minorities. Some scholars, like Aubry and Tribalat (2009), use the national origin of the parents as a substitute for ethnicity. In fact, as duly noted by a bystander during the riots, "in Clichy-sous-Bois, there are three main communities, the Arabs, the Turks and the Black people. The three victims represent each one of them" (*Le Monde*, November 7, 2005).

French sociologists have described the suburbs in the Seine-St-Denis department as pauperized territories, symbols of a social and racial fracture in French society, a fragmentation at the periphery of Paris, where exclusion is a common experience to the residents. French scholars (Lagrange and Oberti, 2006; Castel, 2007; Mucchielli, 2009) argue that the 2005 riots made it abundantly clear that racism, ethnic, and racial discrimination of stigmatized populations were the issues at the heart of the events. Castel (2007) more specifically explains that the populations in the suburbs like Clichy-sous-Bois have been systematically excluded from French society through mechanisms of institutional discrimination and segregation. In particular, scholars (Weil, 2005; Castel, 2007; Schneider, 2008; Simiti, 2012) show that racial minorities in suburbs like the Seine-St-Denis department experience high unemployment rates, discrimination in the labor market, police brutality and abuse, racial profiling, lack of access to adequate healthcare, political exclusion, and spatial isolation. In fact, one of the ways in which geographic exclusion takes place is demonstrated in the fact that Clichy-sous-Bois has no direct connection to Paris by subway or the train Réseau Express Régional (RER, or Regional Express Network), as do other wealthier suburbs of Paris. For the residents of Clichy-sous-Bois, the bus is the only form of public transport granting them access to the next town, where an RER train then takes them to Paris. For Murray (2006), it is no accident that the riots occurred and mostly stayed in the suburbs: "[T]o target more significant symbols of the state would have meant taking a couple of buses and a commuter train to first reach them," Murray (2006: 29) explains.

Media reports and studies by French sociologists produced during and after the riots have identified the populations that participated in the riots. Hugo Lagrange (Lagrange and Oberti, 2006) explains that the rioters were young men (15–20 years old), residents of the suburbs where the riots took place, and that some of them were foreign nationals but the majority were French (only around 7 percent of the arrested rioters were foreign nationals; Roy, 2005). Lagrange (Lagrange and Oberti, 2006) also reports that 26 percent were not enrolled in school, 44 percent had a general studies or technical studies high school degree, and that most were unemployed. Finally, contrary to Sarkozy's initial declarations, most of the rioters (60 percent) did not have any prior criminal record (Lagrange and Oberti, 2006).

The grammar of the White racial frame
Kärcher and racaille

This chapter contends that the physical violence that took place on the streets between rioters and police forces was matched only by the violence of the language used by French government officials and others. According to French sociologist Bourdieu (1979), language can be seen as symbolic capital exerting symbolic violence: for example, he argues that social classes are dominated even and especially in the production of their social image and their social identity. Subjugated classes don't get to speak but are spoken about and against. Applying Bourdieu to the present case, only those with political power and capital are authorized to say what the riots are and how we should think about them and the rioters. As Demiati (2007: 58) explains, the use and radicalization of "unrestrained words" against the rioters and the riots constructed a social reality in the mind of the public that equates to symbolic violence in political discourse.

Even prior to the riots, from the moment Sarkozy was nominated as minister of interior in June 2005, he made many impatient, angry statements about urban security, about the youth of the suburbs (in cities like Perpignan in southern France or La Courneuve, a suburb of Paris) in order to disavow any legitimacy to grievances or complaints by the youths who live in those suburbs (Demiati, 2007: 58–76). For example, in June 2005, while visiting projects in La Courneuve, Sarkozy had claimed that the suburbs should be "cleaned up with a kärcher" (pressure washer). Although the comment did not directly initiate the riots that took place later in October that same year, this kind of expression not only stigmatizes the youth of the suburbs into deviant outsiders and the suburbs as unclean spaces but it also constructs a meta-narrative and a social reality, or a T-discourse, in the words of Dorothy Smith (1993), in the mind of the public about the suburbs and their inhabitants. Smith (1993: 51) argues that T-discourses can be thought of as ideological codes "hooked into policy and political practices." T-discourses organize the activities and practices of individuals. According to Smith (1993), the ideological code found in T-discourses orders the ways that syntax, categories, and vocabulary are chosen and produced. The following examines the racial framing constructed by the French government about the riots and the rioters.

The riots and the rioters as criminal

As soon as the riots began on October 27, 2005, using the same kind of unrestrained words he had used in prior months, then-Minister of Interior Sarkozy commented on the events by denouncing the actions of the rioters, whom he labeled "scum" and "thugs" (the now-infamous French word *racaille*). Sarkozy's derogatory comments almost immediately received a furious reply from then-colleague Delegate Minister for the Promotion of the Equality of Chances/Opportunity Azouz Begag, who stated that "you don't say to young people that they are thugs, you don't say to young people that you're going to attack them and then send them the police" (*Le Monde*, November 1, 2005). Addressing more specifically Sarkozy's comment on cleaning the suburbs with a *kärcher*, Begag added, "I would use the expression 'to clean' or 'clean up' to clean my shoes, my car. I don't 'clean' the *quartiers*" (*Le Monde*, November 1, 2005). Begag also declared that: "When one nominates a Muslim *préfet*, when one claims wanting to grant the right to vote to foreigners, and when one is sending the CRS against the youths in the suburbs, there is a disconnect ... It's by fighting against discriminations" (*Le Monde*, November 1, 2005). Generally, Begag denounced the war semantics Sarkozy used during the riots. However, Begag was struck silent by his own government for being too critical of the government's response to the riots (Wihtol de Wenden, 2005). Despite the numerous criticisms Sarkozy received in response to his comments, not only did he not retract his words but he doubled down on his position by adding more derogatory words and repeating them. On November 6, while visiting with police forces in a northern suburb of Paris, he warned that if the republican order was not soon reestablished, "it will either be the order of the gangs, or the order of the mafias, or another kind of order" (*Le Monde*, November 6, 2005). Sarkozy also denounced the supposed status quo that had prevailed under prior governments by saying that "it has been thirty or forty years that 'things' have been tolerated that should have never been accepted" (*Le Monde*, November 6, 2005). On November 10, Sarkozy made an appearance on French television (during a special news program on France 2) saying that he "insists and persists" in using the words "racaille" and "scum," for, according to him, "one must call a cat a cat" (*Le Monde*, November 11, 2005). He further declared on national television:

> I would like anyone to tell to my face, someone who hits a firefighter, who throws stones to a firefighter, how do we call him? "Young man?" "Sir?" We call him a thug because it's a thug. When I say they are scum [*racaille*], they call themselves that! Stop calling them "young people"! (*Le Monde*, November 11, 2005)

On November 21, in front of about 2,000 new members of his party, the Union pour un Mouvement Populaire (UMP, or Union for Popular Movement), Sarkozy used those terms again, adding, in an ironic tone, that "this vocabulary was perhaps a bit too weak" (*Le Monde*, November 21, 2005). As if to bring evidence to his claim, Sarkozy declared that "the first cause of despair in the *banlieues* is not discrimination. The first cause of despair in the *banlieues* is drug trafficking, the law of the gangs, and the dictatorship of fear" (*Le Monde*, November 21, 2005, emphasis added). Later, in December 2005, Sarkozy affirmed that "75% to 80%" of the rioters were notorious delinquents.

As argued by Feagin (2010b), frame elements are often clustered in key sub-frames within a broad, overarching frame. In this case, one of the central sub-frames here is the criminalization of the rioters, as well as the association and correlation between rioters, urban violence, immigrants, and racial minorities. This criminalization of the rioters is constructed in opposition to the "good" French citizens who are viewed as the victims of the riots. Indeed, using Feagin's (2010b) concept of White racial frame, this chapter argues that Sarkozy's discourse about the rioters rested on racial stereotypes and narratives, as well as emotions, particularly a negative orientation with a feeling of inferiority toward the outgroup (the rioters), and a positive orientation with a feeling of superiority of the dominant in-group (constructed as "White French citizens").

On the one hand, Sarkozy showed empathy to the "good" citizens of the suburbs while, on the other, stigmatizing ethnic minorities, using the double label of "ethnic" and "deviant" in the same sentence so that it became their joined identity. The way that Sarkozy ranked people into categories of "good" ("White" being the sub-text) people who inhabit the suburbs and are the "victims" of the riots on the one hand, and "bad" ethnic/immigrant youths (with the additional label of Islamism and Islamic terrorism) who committed urban violence on the other, allowed him to build a dichotomy, an opposition constructing the rioters as a threat to the republican order and to national identity. In fact, Castel (2007: 61) claims that over the course of the riots, the main question addressed by Sarkozy and the government in their public declarations was the return to order, and that the question of insecurity was framed as the major problem of the suburbs, linking immigration and issues of insecurity. Though to be fair, this isn't all new in Sarkozy's discourse: he has used correlations between ethnicity/nationality and urban violence and criminality before. Additionally, the rhetoric of insecurity and fear associated with the ethnic youths of the suburbs that dominated Sarkozy's language is a well-known form of populist discourse used by the National Front. For example, Noiriel (2007b) explains that a term like *racaille* has been used before, but only by the "hard" right wing during the 1930s. However, over the course of the riots, Sarkozy used derogatory adjectives and nouns, sending a double signal to the White people and to the racial minorities of the suburbs that he was the number one cop of France and that, as such, he was not afraid of being "tough" to preserve and secure the republican order, which is then assumed to be White. As shown by Feagin (2010b), in the United States, "Americans" is routinely used to mean "White Americans," and an expression like "American Dream" is often used to refer to the values and ideals of White people. Similarly, the "big picture narrative" (Feagin, 2010b: 13) of the republican order refers to a society of hardworking White French citizens threatened by racial minorities portrayed by Sarkozy as criminal outsiders from within. More specifically, during the riots Sarkozy used the police doctrine and denounced a youth culture in the suburbs that is, according to Sarkozy, prone to be violent and anti-establishment, or a network of drug dealers, gang leaders, and Islamists. At the same time, Sarkozy and the government in general remained cautious and evasive about the tear gas grenade that was thrown in the direction of a local mosque (which had many worshipers, especially because it was almost the end of Ramadan), and instead focused on the inhabitants of the area who told him "we can't stand it anymore, we're afraid." Olivier Ferrand (2012) argues that Sarkozy's communication strategy was to focus on finding scapegoats to feed to the masses.

This chapter claims that part of this strategy was to establish a racial frame separating an "us" – the good White citizens, victims of the riots – from "them" – immigrants, Muslims, "scum" of the suburbs, delinquents, all grouped in the same collective stigmatized entity. Moran (2011) argues that terms such as "scum," "thug," "youths of the suburbs," all packed together in expressions employed by Sarkozy, create a direct correlation between those labeled and stereotyped individuals who are in the suburbs (that is, racial minorities) and the idea of threat from within to French society. The focus on correlating immigrants/ethnicity/delinquency/urban violence is in that regard part of a larger racial framing that is both racist and nationalist. Here again, using Feagin's (2010b) notion of racial framing, I argue that the criminalization sub-frame used by the French government, which contains all negative elements targeting ethnic and racial minorities in the suburbs, serves as the central reference point. This point of reference then becomes everyone's "frame of mind," the lens through which French citizens make sense of the riots. More specifically, we can see two ways in which the rioters and their actions were delegitimized: one, Sarkozy (and the police who were under his authority) constructed an image of the riots as the actions of organized thugs and gangs of the suburbs, which puts them outside of the institutionally approved means of protests. As shown by Jennifer Eberhardt et al (2004: 876–93), the verbal and visual dehumanization of racial minorities supports the targeting of some groups through societal "cruelty, social degradation, and state-sanctioned violence." Indeed, Sarkozy's rhetoric helped justify a warlike discourse that was calling for the eradication and the cleansing of the scum, and of the suburbs themselves as the perceived menacing social space.

Using Smith's concept of T-discourse (1993), I contend that Sarkozy produced an ideological code through the racial framing of the riots that helped justify in the public eye the use of police violence and state repression against the rioters. As Feagin (2010b) underlines, powerful frames and sub-frames like these include emotions, visual images, and language: as demonstrated here, these verbal elements become the dominant racial frame constructed to rationalize racist discourses and practices. And two, the rhetoric supported by the French government (including Sarkozy), but also by French intellectuals and the media during the riots, presented the suburbs (*quartiers sensibles*) as a menace to the rest of French society. The populations (and the rioters) in the suburbs were labeled as the responsible agents fragmenting the Republic "along ethnocultural lines" (Moran, 2008: 3). The fear that Sarkozy's rhetoric was feeding into has to do with an idea of communitarianism based on racial, ethnic, or religious identities, constructed in opposition to the republican order that implies being a French and White citizen. This Manichean opposition between racial minorities and White French citizens reinforces racist stereotypes describing racial minorities in the suburbs (and, by extension, the suburbs themselves) as the outsiders from within bringing violence and destruction against the "good" citizens of France, a racial frame that has been used by the conservative/right-wing National Front. However, the division constructed by Sarkozy relies on racial codes advancing a colorblind frame that allowed him to use racist discourse "without sounding racist," as Bonilla-Silva (2006) would argue. So, for example, terms such as "gang members" or "extremists" are racial code words for "North African" or "Muslim," also mixed with references to immigration and Islam presented as threats from within. The purpose of such a colorblind racist frame is to seek wide public support from citizens who would not necessarily support the National Front's openly racist rhetoric. By virtue of this framing, presenting the riots as menacing the social order of the "good citizens," the government effectively denied any legitimacy or legitimate meaning to the rioters and their plight. However, Sebastian Roché (2006) notes that representatives of the law would often contradict Sarkozy's presumptions about the rioters and the riots. For example, the implicit association made by Sarkozy regarding the status of the rioters (for example, that 80 percent of the youths brought before the prosecution were well known to the police) has been disproven by the courts and the Direction Centrale des Renseignements Généraux (DCRG, or Central Direction of General Intelligence), which showed that most of the rioters who were arrested had no criminal history. Additionally, while Sarkozy and others claimed the involvement of radical Islam, the DCRG again denied any involvement of radical Muslim groups. In fact, the DCRG reported that Muslim fundamentalists had no role in starting the riots or in the subsequent violence. The DCRG rectified or contradicted Sarkozy's and the government's declarations on several occasions, not only about the status, the numbers, and so on but also about the interpretation of the riots. For example, the report presented by the DCRG in November 2005 called the events "riots" instead of "urban violence" (as the government had qualified them) and declared that the riots represented a "crisis more serious" than random acts of urban violence, diagnosing them as a "popular uprising." In fact, the DCRG report clearly establishes that it was the "social condition of being excluded from society" that was at the source of the rioters' actions. The report further adds that "to limit the events to simple urban violence would be an error of analysis." The DCRG report, as published in *Le Monde* (December 7, 2005), also claims that "the youths from the 'sensible' areas feel penalized by poverty, by the color of their skin and by their names" and that they are handicapped by "the absence of perspectives in French society." The report concludes that the riots were the result of a deep sense of social despair felt by the youths in the suburbs, as well as a "total loss of confidence in the Republic." Nonetheless, Sarkozy's racial framing of the rioters helped him and the government justify a particular social order where disenfranchised individuals and communities experience oppression and are held responsible for their social conditions. What Sarkozy's rhetoric accomplished through its hegemony was to enable the government to deny the individuals any legitimacy in their fight against oppression, any agency in publicly ascribing their own meanings to their fight. Sarkozy's racial framing functioned as an ideological code, a T-discourse permeating the formulation of texts and actions against the rioters. Power thus manifests itself with the creation of a dominant ideology through a rhetoric that guides and justifies actions and policies, as seen subsequently.

The state of emergency and colonial legacy

Sarkozy's racial framing of the rioters allowed him to deny any legitimacy and meaning to the riots. It also enabled him to rationalize the use of repressive measures, like the state of emergency. As argued by Pascal-Yan Sayegh (2008: 10), policies can be analyzed as "discursive elements that provide additional support to a discourse." On November 4, 2005, then vice president of the far-right party Front National (or National Front) Marine Le Pen, daughter of then-party leader Jean-Marie Le Pen, requested the imposition of a state of emergency. In her statement, she pointed out that the measures had been used in 1985 by then-French President François Mitterrand "to reestablish the republican order in New-Caledonia, for troubles that were infinitely less serious than today" (*Le Monde*, November 4, 2005).

On November 7, Prime Minister Dominique de Villepin announced that the government would put in place the state of emergency law from 1955, especially using the curfew regulation. At this point, this was the first official speech given by the head of the government since the start of the riots. He authorized the *préfets* to start imposing a curfew by November 9. On November 8, French President Jacques Chirac confirmed that he would apply the 1955 law declaring a state of emergency for the country. On November 9, the declaration of an emergency state that the government had adopted the day before took effect with the publication of a simple decree by Minister of Interior Sarkozy in the *Journal Officiel*. It applied to the continental territory of France (or the *métropole*), where it had never been used before.

The state of emergency law of April 3, 1955 was adopted for the Algerian War (when Algeria was a French colony). According to this law, the government can declare a state of emergency by decree for a maximum length of 12 days. It was used in Algeria in 1955 to reestablish social order and then again in 1985 in New Caledonia for the same reason, in both cases as a system of repression against subjugated groups. More specifically, as explained by Sylvie Thénault (2007), the state of emergency law was used in 1955 against colonized Algerians to prevent them from starting a war of independence, and it was also used in 1985 in New Caledonia against the Kanak independence movement in the context of independence uprisings. In the case of the 2005 riots more specifically, Article 5 of the law gives power to the *préfets* (with the agreement of the mayor of each city to which it is applied) to enforce a curfew; to impose an interdiction of stay or summons home stay to people causing troubles; to order the closure of public places (including cafés, bars, restaurants, cinemas, conference centers, and so on); to ban any meetings or gatherings of people that might provoke or perpetuate disorder; to proceed with house searches night or day without any warrant; and to control the press, among other things. During the riots, 25 departments were affected by the state of emergency law of 1955; six departments applied it, and four departments still had it in place in December 2005. For the state of emergency law to remain in place beyond 12 days (that is, beyond November 20), the decision needed to be voted into law by the National Assembly, the lower house of the bicameral Parliament of France. On November 15, prior to the vote, Sarkozy made a speech at the National Assembly to defend his proposal to extend the state of emergency law for three more months. Using a rhetoric of fear, he declared: "15 minutes away from the center of Paris … cars are burning," and then again, "15 minutes away from the center of Paris … there are French people who look down walking in the street and triple lock their doors when they get home, and live in fear, and it's been a few years like that already." And finally, Sarkozy said: "[T]he time for truth has come! … Because if it is not the order of the Republic that reigns in these areas, it will be the order of the gangs or the extremists." Here again, Sarkozy used code words like "gangs" or "extremists" to mean "North African," "Black," or "Muslim," referring to residents of projects in suburbs like Clichy-sous-Bois. Such code words allowed Sarkozy to construct negative connotations about racial minorities using a colorblind racist discourse. Using Smith's (1993) concept, Sarkozy's code words can be analyzed as ideological codes transmitting a schema into which descriptive elements can be inserted, creating a dominant racist trope with the appearance of colorblindness. Sarkozy's codes didn't simply justify his own repressive policies; they also normalized and validated the racist rhetoric of the extreme right. Furthermore, the discourse Sarkozy used to justify the application of the emergency law centered on security and how people live in fear, and on all the money given to the *cités*, or the *quartiers*, without tangible or positive results. For him, the "central factor" for what he called urban violence was "the will of those who made delinquent acts their main activity in order to resist the ambition of the Republic for order and law on its territory" (*Le Monde*, November 15, 2005). However, in reaction to Sarkozy's speech, then Green Party representative Noël Mamère declared that "the state of emergency law cannot be the response to a state of social catastrophe" (*Le Monde*, November 16, 2005). Additionally, several organizations publicly showed their disagreement and disapproval of this measure. On November 15, criticizing the application of the state of emergency law, the Syndicat de la Magistrature (French professional union of members of the judiciary) claimed: "Considering the serious detrimental character of such a measure to civil liberties, the international conventions stipulate that the States who choose to apply this law must inform the United Nations' General Secretary as well as the European Council's General Secretary" (*Le Monde*, November 15, 2005). Several human rights associations and civil liberties organizations reacted in a joint statement, saying that "you cannot respond to a social crisis with a regime of exception" and that "there is here a real national emergency, and we must replace this police state of emergency by a state of social emergency, so that the actions of the government stop contradicting the principle of the Republic" (*Le Monde*, November 14, 2005). Nonetheless, the law to extend the state of emergency passed with 346 votes in favor and 148 opposed. The UMP and the Union pour la Démocratie Française party (UDF, or Union for French Democracy) voted in favor, while the Parti Socialiste (or Socialist Party), except for one person, the Parti Communiste (or French Communist Party), and the Greens voted against. On November 16, the French Senate adopted the text extending the emergency law (especially the curfew), even though things were returning to normal and the violence (or reports of violence) had decreased significantly. On November 18, Prime Minister de Villepin declared that he had no intention of lifting the state of emergency law before the beginning of 2006. The vote on the emergency law was made possible by the White racial framing of the riots, which gave Sarkozy and the government a rationalization, if not impunity, for dealing with the riots. Indeed, using the 1955 state of emergency law, which was the first measure brought by the head of the government in dealing with the riots, the French government sent a clear message to the rioters: they would be treated the very same way that their ancestors in Algeria (and in other former colonies) were, that is, through oppression, subjugation, and repression. The rioters had already been construed and treated as outlaws, so, by applying the state of emergency law, they also become de facto "children of the traitors" of yesterday's colonies, claims Rigouste (2011). In that regard, Rigouste (2011: 278) argues, the emergency law carried a "symbolic and memorial" dimension by placing it in the framework of a "pacification of the enemy of the interior." Indeed, the emergency law allowed Sarkozy to use what amounts to warlike operations in some parts of the French territory and against some populations, without having to subject the whole economic and political structure to the same regimen. In that regard, Thénault (2007: 76) argues, the state of emergency law is as much "a law of political repression as it is a colonial law." For Thénault (2007), the idea behind the state of emergency law is to repress anyone who is an outlaw, that is, anyone who is acting outside of and against the republican system of law and order, anyone, in fact, who contests the republican order. Thus anyone who does not recognize the republican order and its laws by acting outside and against it should not expect to receive the guarantees and protection of the common law. On the contrary, anyone acting outside of the law should expect to be treated with a regime of exception, such as the emergency law. Furthermore, Thénault (2007) explains, the emergency law in France is deeply rooted in the larger history of repression in France, primarily directed at populations and movements that are perceived to threaten republican order, like the independence movements in the former colonies. The passage of the emergency law can thus be seen as a racist policy targeting populations that were accused of being outside of the republican contract and its institutions, even though it is precisely the institutions, through institutional racism, that had placed them outside the republican social contract. Rigouste (2011) even goes so far as to suggest that, in some ways, this period of "exception" (since the emergency law is a law of exception) was a good time to experiment for Sarkozy: it had the function of a full-scale social laboratory experiment – a kind of lab to test a new counter-insurgency program that had just been circulated on October 18, 2005. According to Thénault (2007), 73 percent of French people polled by the polling institute CSA approved the proclamation of the state of emergency law. Additionally, on November 9, Sarkozy announced that he had asked the *préfets* to deport all non-French citizens who had committed violent acts or simply participated in the riots, even if they were "legal" foreigners and/or residents by status. Sarkozy specified that 120 foreigners (not necessarily undocumented) had been convicted. On November 14, Sarkozy reiterated that there would soon be some deportations. However, Sarkozy faced difficulties in applying the law, as per Sarkozy's own November 2003 law, because deportations do not apply to minors, or to adults who arrived in France before the age of 13 or who have strong family links in the country. The question of deportations actually undermined a simple fact: the rioters were predominantly French citizens, most of them second generation from immigrant parents; hence, the government could not send them "back" anywhere. But the media hype around the idea of deportations contributed to the construction of a racist narrative about non-French foreign criminals being the main instigators of the riots. Using Gilles Finchelstein's (2011) analysis of the banalization of the ideas of the National Front, by using words like *racaille* or proposing to send the supposed delinquents "back" to their country, Sarkozy was indeed paraphrasing ideas of the National Front, which are based on a populist, nationalist, and racist ideology. Ideas previously used by the extreme right have become "banal" in the political landscape because Sarkozy's rhetoric justified and legitimized the ideology behind them. In the end, then, in line with Feagin's (2010b) concept of White racial framing, the racial framing of the rioters as thugs and criminals by the French government created a negative narrative about their actions, which denied them any legitimacy while normalizing a racist discourse and rationalizing racist policy measures against them.

Cultural racism as colorblind racism

On November 10, on national public television France 2, Sarkozy expressed his views on why some people experience integration problems. Making a covert link between the riots and the rioters, he explained: "There are more problems for a kid of an immigrant from Black Africa or North Africa than for a son of a Swedish, Danish or Hungarian.15 Because of culture, because of polygamy, because social origins make it more difficult" (*Le Monde*, November 10, 2005). The "polygamy case," as presented by Sarkozy, was also used by then-Minister of Employment Gérard Larcher, who declared that polygamy was one of the explanations for racial discrimination in the workforce and one of the main causes for the violent urban uprisings; according to him, polygamy represented a "disintegration of family values" (*Le Monde*, November 15, 2005). On November 7, Prime Minister de Villepin declared that some "criminal networks are supporting the chaos" in the suburbs and called for "responsibility from the parents." Following this statement, on November 14, the Mayor of Draveil (a city southeast of Paris), Georges Tron, announced that he would immediately suspend social aid to families of rioters in his commune. These family allocations include aid for food, utilities, rent, school dinners, vacations for children, medical prescriptions, and phone bills. On the same day, the Minister of State for Family Affairs, Philippe Bas, indicated that there was a discussion taking place about a law that would suspend any family allocations/aid to parents who did not "carry out correctly their parental function/duty" (*Le Monde*, November 14, 2005). The problem with such an argument about parental responsibility was that it completely ignored the fact that families in these suburbs had been facing a social and economic strain – structural violence – for over 20 years, which had broken any "normal" way of functioning, if there even existed such a thing. Finally, in an interview with French magazine *l'Express* on November 17, Sarkozy said: "[Those rioters] are totally French legally speaking. But let's say things as they really are: polygamy, the acculturation of a number of families makes it more difficult to integrate a young individual of African origin than another young French person of another origin."

In addition to declarations by political officials, some French intellectuals commented on the riots using a similar White racial frame regarding the rioters and the idea of threat against the "Republic." Specifically, François Gèze (2006: 89) talks about the "fundamentalists of the Republic," an intellectual nebula of thinkers who have been vocal about the riots. Murray (2006: 32) also refers to this group or movement of French scholars called the *néoréacs*, or neo-reactionaries, for which the equivalent in the United States would be the "neocons," who have professed their own perspective on the events using arguments similar to those employed by the far right, although they have defended themselves against being described as racists. Their declarations usually share two points: the defense of republican principles they deem essential, and the supposed resistance to the invasion of "barbarians" that are usually portrayed as immigrants and/or Muslims. For example, renowned French scholar Hélène Carrère d'Encausse, an expert on Russia, declared in the Russian media that "if so many African children are loitering around in the street," then it was because "many of these Africans are polygamists" (Carrère d'Encausse, 2005). However, Carrère d'Encausse offered no evidence to support her argument. Literary theorist Tzvetan Todorov declared at a conference at Columbia University that the riots "were caused by the dysfunctional sexuality of Muslim youth obsessed with behaving in a macho way" (Hargreaves, 2005). Additionally, in an interview with the Israeli newspaper *Haaretz* (November 18, 2005), French philosopher Alain Finkielkraut explained that the "problem" was that "most of these young people are black or Arabs and have a Muslim identity." Finkielkraut frames the riots in terms of hate stemming from the culture and the religion (Islam) of the rioters against a Judeo-Christian tradition in France. In addition to public intellectuals like Finkielkraut correlating the presence of Islam in France with danger, Castel (2007: 54) claims that over the past several years the French government has increased its public declarations on Islam, framing Islam as a potential threat to the Republic and its universal values. In the 2005 *Haaretz* interview, Finkielkraut further states that there were in France "other immigrants in difficult situations – Chinese, Vietnamese, Portuguese – and they don't participate in the riots. Therefore, it is clear that this revolt is ethnic and religious in character."

The word "immigrant" used in many of these declarations is a euphemism for race, blurring any distinctive identity between Black, North African or Arab people. Maxim Silverman (1992: 37) explains that although racial minorities in France "do not appear statistically as foreigners, they are frequently classified popularly as immigrants because of the racialized association between immigration, those of North African origin, and blacks." Additionally, contrary to the prejudiced commentaries by the intellectuals cited above, and per the findings of the French intelligence service, Islam or radical Islam did not play any role at all in the riots. In fact, as noted by Cathy Schneider (2008), imams from the major mosques actually implored the youths to stay calm. In many ways, a part of the Parisian intellectual class basically supported Sarkozy's use of derogatory language, arguing that the riots were simply a fire of hatred fanned by delinquents, and that Sarkozy was the victim of misplaced and wrongful criticisms from the left.

As explained by Bonilla-Silva (2006), colorblind racism is a set of frameworks that help explain and justify the racial status quo without having to specifically refer to race. It is a racial ideology that allows for rationalizations and justifications of a racial order based on explanations other than race and in that regard minimizes the relevance and significance of race. During and after the riots, the focus of the discourse on foreigners (who have become scapegoats), the accusation against the parents (guilty of being poor and excluded), and an intensified accusatory language focused on the threat of Islam against law and order is a perfect illustration of Bonilla-Silva's concept of cultural racism. One of the central frames of colorblind racism is cultural racism, which uses cultural arguments to explain racial-ethnic minorities' positions in society. It "blames the victim" by attempting to identify cultural aspects of minorities and by explaining that they are inferior to the White normative culture. Therefore, their deficient culture is identified as the source of their inability to succeed. As Bonilla-Silva (2006: 29) claims, this is "racism without racists." The rhetoric of Sarkozy, the French government, and others in the media and part of the French intellectual class, through stereotypes and stigmas, showed complete contempt and disregard of the riots as a political act, and of the rioters and their plight. Moreover, the use of such derogatory language allowed Sarkozy to define and construct an image of the rioters as delinquents and put the blame directly on the rioters and their families for their own plight, which is one of the arguments of cultural racism. Indeed, based on Bonilla-Silva's analysis of colorblind racism, we can see here how the use of cultural claims to explain the status of racial minorities in French society allowed the government to essentially "blame the victims" by identifying cultural aspects constructed as inferior to the White normative culture, without using an explicit racial discourse. As Bonilla-Silva (2006) and Wieviorka (1998) show, the biological views that previously supported explicit racial ideologies are replaced by cultural ones in contemporary racism. Using cultural racism, Minister of Interior Sarkozy and members of the government delegitimized the rioters' plight by framing them as a dangerous, culturally deviant class, which gave Sarkozy the authority to employ an alarming rhetoric of fear and chaos in order to justify confrontation and repression. As Castel (2007: 61) notes, no mediation was ever offered during the riots. Sarkozy's criminalization narrative against the rioters based on their presumed cultural deficiencies gave him full legitimacy to apply security measures in much the same way as a police state. The rhetoric used by Sarkozy and other representatives of the French government also shows an ideological alignment with the thesis of the ideas of the far-right party National Front, including anti-immigrant rhetoric and xenophobia. Indeed, Michel Tubiana (2006) suggests that the government has used the rhetoric of the National Front in a more open and uninhibited way that stigmatizes foreigners and puts the guilt and responsibility exclusively on the parents of the rioters, linking a parental deficit to their culture. Using Bonilla-Silva's concept of cultural racism (2006: 40), this chapter argues that focusing on questions about Islam or the family structure, and connecting them directly to the riots and urban violence, is an ideological banalization of the racist and populist ideas of the National Front, making them appear a normal and banal expression of political analysis of French society.

Conclusion

Most French social scientists have admitted that the 2005 riots were not a new phenomenon in the contentious politics of the French suburbs. In fact, Laurent Bonelli (2005) qualifies the riots as "an ordinary mode of protest." Indeed, Bonelli (2005) points out that the particular "practice" of burning cars had already occurred, in 2003, when about 21,500 vehicles were burned in the course of the year (representing an average of 60 cars per night). However, if the methods of contention were not original, the length of this particular type of protest and the demographics of the participants were a somewhat new phenomenon. Laurent Mucchielli (2009: 732) thus claims that the 2005 French riots were France's "most consequential riots in its contemporary history." Many scholars, like Eric Marlière (2011), have pointed out that the riots were definitely not a form of "unmotivated violence." Similarly, Marilena Simiti (2012: 145) argues that despite being "volatile," the riots were not "irrational, random and unorganized events." Rather, they can be analyzed as contentious events challenging existing norms and policies. As Denis Merklen (2006: 131) suggests, the mobilization of November 2005 consisted of political acts: "[S]ometimes, burning cars is a matter of politics, as much as calling the ones who have done it 'delinquents' is an act of political dismissal."

Yet, the ethnic riots of 2005 have not been treated as political acts by the French government, the media, or by some French intellectuals but rather as a deviation from the norm in terms of political behavior. In fact, the 2005 riots have been framed by the government, the media, and certain public intellectuals as an attack, or a threat, against French republican democratic order. However, some scholars (Weil, 2005; Hargreaves, 2005; Castel, 2007; Fassin and Fassin, 2009; Simiti, 2012) have instead focused on the issues of racism, equal rights, justice, and opportunities. Such scholars view the riots not as a menace to the French Republic but rather as confronting the behavior of political leaders who continuously delegitimized their voice (and who may well be the ones "acting in an 'unrepublican' manner"), as well as questioning the treatment to which they are subjected in their daily lives, including being denied access to republican citizenship.

Through this chapter, I have examined the pattern of the state response to the riots that took place in the French suburbs in 2005. Using Bonilla-Silva's (2006) colorblind racism framework, and Feagin's (2010b, 2012) White racial framing perspective, this chapter has shown that (1) by discrediting the rioters themselves through a White racial rhetorical framework, the French government denied any legitimacy to the riots; and that (2) through a colorblind racist framing of the rioters, the state rationalized and justified its own repressive acts and measures, calling for an even more oppressive rhetoric, all of which further neutralized the voice of the rioters. Indeed, the stigmatization of the rioters as criminals and the "enemy from within" allowed the government to deny all political meaning and legitimacy to their motives. The government – particularly the Minister of Interior Nicolas Sarkozy – used "a particular language and rhetoric to make 'colorblind' arguments and denigrate oppressed groups" (Byrd, 2011: 1007). In essence, Sarkozy's stigmatizing rhetoric denied the very existence of the social conditions in which the participants found themselves every day, which were at the root and core of the riots. By giving a hegemonic reading on the riots, Sarkozy and the French government in particular were supporting a dominant racist ideology that could not be challenged by the rioters, who had no rhetorical agency. As residents of the *banlieues*, the rioters already experienced domination in their everyday practices (discrimination, police brutality, segregation, unemployment, poverty), but also in the production of their social image. In the case of the riots, because of their lack of rhetorical agency, the rioters did not get to participate in the construction of the social reality – they didn't get to present a counterhegemonic discourse about the riots because there is no negotiated or oppositional reading at work (Hall, 1993). As Lagrange (2006: 55) explains, the rioters, who were already marginalized and oppressed in their everyday social experiences, were also isolated politically. The rioters then have the least control over the production of a discourse about their social reality. Sarkozy and the French government, on the other hand, emitted a T-discourse (Smith, 1993), an ideological code asserting dominant claims about the reality of the riots that in turn governed the political decisions and policies toward the rioters.

Furthermore, not only did Sarkozy and the French government exert symbolic violence upon dominated social agents (Bourdieu, 1979) through the imposition of categories of thought but they also imposed the specter of legitimacy of a racist social order. Sarkozy's hegemonic discourse reduced the rioters' and the public's agency because it limited the choices of analysis that give meaning and interpretation. Racialized framing of riots isn't exclusive to France, and scholars (Hunt, 1997; Messer and Bell, 2010) have shown that media and government in the United States have used a White racial frame to stigmatize nonWhite rioters as criminals. Other studies (Cavanagh and Dennis, 2012) have looked at the framing of the 1981 riots in the UK and how the riots were also coded in terms of race and race relations. However, Harlan Koff and Dominique Duprez (2009: 723) claim that, unlike the United States and Great Britain, "France has not attempted to find solutions to the problems that caused the 2005 riots." Instead, Koff and Duprez (2009: 723) argue, Sarkozy and the French government actually benefited from the riots in that by racializing the riots and criminalizing the rioters, they were able to justify more anti-immigrant campaigns and restrictive citizenship policies, attracting the conservative electorate from the far-right party, National Front. Additionally, as observed by French sociologist Macé (2005), blaming the rioters without relating the riots to their larger socioeconomic conditions amounts to "accusing the rioters of the Commune of Paris in 1870 who revolted against the bourgeoisie which had made alliance with the German troops occupying France," or denouncing the violence "perpetrated by the natives during the decolonization wars." By comparison, when French farmer José Bové dismantled a McDonald's in 1999, and was sentenced to prison for it, or when Green activists regularly destroyed transgenic crops in the fields, they received the support of the French public and the media. In some cases, people even protested to show their support of the activists. Furthermore, in March 2006, and hence shortly after the October 2005 ethnic riots, students (mostly White and middle class) protested in the streets in the heart of Paris, close to the university La Sorbonne, against a government employment reform called Contrat Première Embauche (CPE or First Hire Contract) affecting students entering the job market. Although they too burned cars in the center of Paris, the student protesters were presented in a positive light by the media as a "political generation," in contrast to the coverage of the 2005 riots on the outskirts of Paris. In the end, not only did they receive public support but they eventually succeeded in their demand, as the French government backed down and dropped the reform altogether. Generally, Macé (2005) stresses, when union workers (mostly composed of White people) oppose the French government through strikes and sometimes violent confrontations – as was the case during the major protests of 1995 and the massive transport strikes of 2007 – the damage caused to public or private property (such as cars) do not reduce or negate the significance of the struggle itself. In fact, such contentious acts have been explained and even justified in terms of structural arrangements in French society. Such was not the case in the November 2005 riots. Koff and Duprez (2009) argue that French leaders and citizens have "distanced themselves from the discontent that led to the riots." Bleich et al (2010), who focus on the state response to riots in Western Europe, explain that different response patterns can be identified according to the levels of repression and accommodation used by the states in question. In comparing ethnic riots in the UK (Brixton in 1981 and Bradford in 2001) and in France (Lyon in 1990 and Paris in 2005), they find that states employ repression and/or accommodation depending on two factors – social control and electoral incentives. For the 2005 ethnic riots in Paris, they claim that high repression and medium accommodation was employed by the French government, whereas the 1990 ethnic riots in Lyon provoked low repression and high accommodation. They argue that the electoral incentives model accounts for the differences: in particular, the political landscape explains the differences in state response, where a left government in the 1990 riots showed low repression and high accommodation, and a right-wing government in the 2005 riots responded with high repression. Further comparative studies looking at the racial framing of riots in different national cases would be useful, particularly in the context of the strong progression of the far right in Europe, but such an analysis goes beyond the immediate scope of the current chapter and demands further research.

The rhetoric used during the riots by the French government – Sarkozy, as well as some of the French intellectual class – largely corresponded to an ideological meta-narrative that is both racist and nationalist and has served as the validation and banalization of far-right views. Using Feagin's approach (2010b), this chapter has demonstrated that the White racial framing used by the French government has become hegemonic, as it normalizes the language and interpretations that make sense of social arrangements. In line with Sayegh's work (2008) showing Sarkozy's contribution to a dominant culturalist discourse on identity in Europe, Sarkozy's rhetoric and policies during the 2005 riots can be analyzed as a White racial framing of the identity of the rioters, who were constructed as "non-French," immigrants, or foreigners. By applying a colorblind frame onto the riots and the rioters, Sarkozy legitimized and banalized a racist and populist narrative that has been used by the National Front, albeit without sounding racist, because his seemingly nonracial framing focused on a concern over the threat and menace that the rioters supposedly brought to the entire French Republic. Noiriel (2008) argues that this kind of rhetoric is part of a larger "populist shift in contemporary political communication." This should raise some serious concerns, because, as Wieviorka (1998) explains, populist and extreme right parties in France, Italy, Austria, and Belgium have become important political forces to be reckoned with as they have gained in electoral support by using racist and anti-Semitic ideologies. Europe witnessed the entrance into the Swedish Parliament of the extreme right party (the Sverigedemokraterna) as a result of Sweden's 2010 general elections and the strong reemergence of the extreme right party in Austria (the Freiheitliche Partei Österreichs) in the October 2010 regional elections. Additionally, the right-wing populist Norwegian party Framstegspartiet made its first entrance into the Norwegian government in October 2013 and is now in a position of strength and power, 40 years after its creation. In light of these political changes, the radicalization of Sarkozy's discourse against racial minorities doesn't seem like an isolated outlier. It may even indicate a trend among other European parties and nations to integrate the "extreme" into their "right" and further normalize and legitimize state racism at home.

6

Islam and the Republic

In a 2015 interview on French public television (France 2), member of the conservative party Les Républicains and elected member at the European Parliament Nadine Morano stated: "[I]n order to have a national cohesion, we must keep an equilibrium in the country, meaning one's own cultural majority. We are a Judeo-Christian country, as General de Gaulle said it, of white race. I want France to remain France. I don't want France to become Muslim."

In a 2016 speech, Sarkozy, then conservative candidate for the 2017 French presidential elections, declared that "wearing a burkini is a political act, militant, a provocation. Women who wear them are testing the resistance of the Republic. Doing nothing is to let everyone think that France appears weak, and it would be like showing a new setback for the Republic" (*Le Monde*, August 24, 2016). During that period, the presence of the burkini – a portmanteau word made of burqa and bikini, a type of swimsuit for women, which in some cases is worn to respect Islamic traditions of modest dress – had provoked heated public debates for weeks, and more than 30 French cities, including Cannes and Nice, had passed city decrees forbidding them from being worn in public spaces, such as beaches.

Both comments, like many other public declarations made by French politicians about Muslims or Islam in France, convey the fact that Muslim or Islam is used as a racialized category, a euphemism for race, and that such a category is located in opposition and as a threat to what is presented as the true roots of France and French identity, as well as social stability. Additionally, it is an indirect way to refer to another culturally and ideologically significant element of French national identity, namely *laïcité* (roughly translated as secularism), a law primarily about the separation of church and state but that has come to be at the center of ferocious debates and declarations about Islam in France. Thus, when examining the performativity of colorblindness in France, we must turn to the framing of *laïcité* as legally enshrined secularism, which makes religion both a gatekeeper to the assertion of French identity and a marker for ethno-racial outsiders like Muslims in France.

This chapter exposes the problematic narratives and racial framing linked to the promotion of the *laïcité* principle, of the universalist feminism frame, and the idea of republican free speech, all frames that racialize Islam in France and perpetuate discrimination against French Muslims, particularly women. The chapter will also review the different regulations in Europe, as compared with France, with regard to the Islamic veil.

Muslims in France or French Muslims?

Due to the 1978 law on personal data collection, it is forbidden to ask for someone's religious affiliation in the French census and any other institutional questionnaires. However, INSEE and INED are able to measure the level of religious practice for sociological studies. This probably explains the different estimates that can be found on the number of Muslims in France. Even without being able to establish precise figures with certainty, according to the Observatoire de la Laïcité (Sall, 2019) Muslims are estimated to number about 4.1 million of the total French population (6 percent), whereas in 2017 the Pew Research Center gave an estimate of 5.7 million (8.8 percent). However, an updated survey published by the Observatoire de la Laïcité in 2022 (with the polling institute Viavoice) shows that 37 percent of French people declare having a religious belief, against 31 percent who identify as atheists or nonbelievers and 15 percent agnostics. Among the people who consider themselves believers, 48 percent affiliate as Catholics, 34 percent say they are not affiliated with any religion, and 4 percent affiliate with Islam. In addition, it is estimated that there are between 70,000 and 110,000 converts to Islam, comprising numerous individuals of different cultural, religious, and socioeconomic backgrounds (Downing, 2019). This makes Islam the second religion in France, far behind Catholicism. At the same time, French politicians exaggerate these numbers and come up with their own estimates, closer to 10 or 15 percent of the population, but without citing their sources (notably the Rassemblement National, or RN, leaders for example, but also leaders from conservative parties). Even citing the numbers of Muslims in France is at stake.

In 2000, the French HCI report classified France's Muslim population as comprising Algerians (1.5 million); Moroccans (1 million); Tunisians (500,000); Turks (350,000); other Middle Easterners (400,000); sub-Saharan Africans (250,000).

France is the country with the largest concentration of Muslims in Europe today, most of them being of Maghrebi (North African) origin (Gray, 2008; d'Appolonia, 2009). As explained by Beaman (2016), this is a source of confusion, as regardless of whether or not they identify as Muslims, individuals of Maghrebi origin are often categorized as Muslim in the media and popular culture. What also complicates the matter is that, as shown in previous chapters, this part of North Africa is also where France had a number of colonies (notably Algeria, Tunisia, Morocco), and these are precisely the places where most of the individuals of Maghrebi origin who live in France are from. The colonial past weighs on how the political class, the media, and White French perceive the presence and place of Muslims and Islam in France.

As well as the estimates of the number of Muslims being disputed, with official sources unable to prove or provide accurate numbers, things are rendered yet more complicated by the terminology used to refer to Muslims. Indeed, as underlined by Joseph Downing (2019), the choice of terms can be problematic. Should we talk about Muslims in France or French Muslims? "Muslims in France" seems to indicate that it is an entity separated from the rest of France, as if they resided in France but were not of France. On the other hand, the term "French Muslims" implies that individuals all share the same status when that may not be the case for all, and yet it isn't just about holding a passport either. Thus, when we use the term French Muslims as I do here, we must take care not to essentialize the group "Muslims" or the identity of "being Muslim" and acknowledge that it does not represent a fixed and homogeneous category. In the same way that Frenchness, or "being French," is a construct with a multiplicity of statuses, ideas, practices, symbols, habits, beliefs, and customs, so is being a Muslim, and Islam, which, despite being a universalist religion with somewhat central beliefs and practices, is also composed of singular and particular nuances tied to local contexts in France, as well as being connected to the different experiences of Frenchness.

Muslims and Islam

One issue when examining the discriminatory discourses against Muslims (the people) and Islam (the religion) is that, as noted by Cheng (2015), there is a tendency to conflate and confuse Islamophobia and Muslimophobia. **Since 2015**, terms such as Islamophobia (the most common), Muslimophobia, anti-Muslim racism, anti-Muslim hate, anti-Muslimism, and anti-Muslim prejudice have been used interchangeably, without any differentiation, in the media and public debates (Cheng, 2015).

According to Jörg Stolz (2005: 548), Islamophobia can be defined as the "rejection of Islam, Muslim groups and Muslim individuals on the basis of prejudices and stereotypes." Mattias Gardell (2014: 133) explains that here the suffix "phobia" connotes "socially, culturally, and politically produced prejudices, aversions and discrimination against specific categories of humans, in this case Muslims." However, Cheng (2015) and Burak Erdenir (2010) argue that the phobia does not arise from a theological conflict with the Islamic religion but rather from a secular anti-Muslim sentiment. Thus in this sense, Erdenir (2010) claims that Muslimophobia is a more appropriate and accurate term to describe racist attitudes toward groups and individuals who identify as Muslims. In fact, Cheng (2015) argues, Muslims are racialized in that some cultural characteristics (such as physical appearance, names, and dress like the headscarf or Islamic veil) are constructed as proxies for race and used in racist discourses. In her essay, Cheng (2015) concludes that although Islamophobia does coexist with Muslimophobia, discourse analysis shows that some discourses are more Islamophobic and explicitly hostile toward the religion of Islam.

Mohamad Meziane (2021: 126) goes as far as saying that Islamophobia and the policing of Islam in France demonstrate what he calls "colonial modernity." According to Meziane (2021: 128), the discourse presented and constructed by the media and some politicians in France about the threat of "Islamist separatism" allows the French state to justify and intensify its repression against Muslims through laws and regulations, particularly by "unveiling Muslim women and policing Muslim men."

The expression "Islamist separatism" was used for the first time by French President Macron in the fall of 2019 in a speech after the Paris police headquarters attack where a police employee stabbed six colleagues, and a counter-terrorism investigation determined that the attacker was a radicalized Islamist. A year later, in the fall of 2020, Macron gave a speech explaining his vision of the fight against "Islamist separatism." This speech was followed, on October 16 2020, by the murder of middle school teacher Samuel Paty, who was killed by a perpetrator identified as an Islamist terrorist by the police, an event that intensified public declarations regarding "Islamist separatism."

The French government defines what it calls "Islamist separatism" or the "withdrawal into one's own community [*repli communautaire*]" as

> the will to submit a group or a social space to norms coming from the interpretation of a religion, in this case Islam. This phenomenon leads to an important part of social life being, in effect, organized and controlled by groups with religious inspiration, rigoristic and militant, and for some carrying a political project with ideas of split and secession. (From the Secrétariat général du comité interministériel de prévention de la délinquance et de la radicalisation [SG-CIPDR], or inter-ministerial committee for the prevention of delinquency and radicalization, n.d.)

It is on the basis of this somewhat vague definition that the Minister of Interior enforces the law, which was passed by the French Parliament in July 2021. Some of the aims of the law regarding "Islamist separatism" include "fighting against foreign influence, better organization of the Muslim worship, [and] fighting against all manifestation of Islamist separatism." The law came into effect in January 2022 with five main areas of concern:

1. The reinforcement of the public service.
2. Protection of community associations from Islamist drift.
3. Better protection of individual rights and equal rights between men and women.
4. An increase in resources to fight against online hatred.
5. Updating the principles of worship organization from the December 9, 1905 law.

One result of the law is that in order to continue receiving public funding, associations need to sign a "contract of republican commitment." The law also gives the prefects of each department in the regions of France the authority to go to an administrative judge whenever a local public institution applies measures deemed contrary to *laïcité*: for example, differentiated opening hours at a swimming pool, school lunch menus influenced by religious considerations, renting a city building or space for free to a religious organization (*Le Monde*, January 10, 2022). As a result of this law, according to French newspaper *Le Monde* (January 10, 2022), several dozen Muslim places of worship have been closed, and the government has set up local department committees to fight against Islamism and community withdrawal (Cellules de Lutte contre l'Islamisme Radical et le Repli Communautaire, or CLIR).

The French state's conflation of the notion of "Islamist separatism" and the representation of Muslims as "communities of fear" (Downing, 2019) is made possible by an essentialization process. Indeed, one of the ways through which essentialization supports colorblind racism is by depicting Muslims as a monolithic and coherent group with a fixed essence on the one hand, and more specifically as outsiders and a threat to European values, particularly presumed Judeo-Christian values in France, on the other. The construction of a Judeo-Christian heritage label for France has two implications: first, it allows France to present itself as a Judeo-Christian society and culture while minimizing the presence of anti-Semitism in France. This minimization has in turn become an important feature of French society and ethos, when, as seen in previous chapters, the French state has a history of anti-Semitic policies and laws, and French society has witnessed anti-Semitic acts by individuals and groups throughout its history. Second, it allows France to create a false dichotomy between two essentialized categories. Indeed, this self-proclaimed Judeo-Christian heritage enables France to present Muslims as fundamentally opposed to presumed French Judeo-Christian values by virtue of their religion. Therefore, Muslims are not only viewed as unable to integrate into French society but also as threatening social order in France and as essentially anti-Semitic. Downing (2019) even shows that this fear of Muslim communities spills over into French literature, as seen in Michel Houellebecq's novel *Submission*, which describes France being Islamized. It was also a feature of the 2022 presidential election campaign, in which far-right candidate Eric Zemmour's campaign talking points were based, among other things, on the idea that he intended to "protect French identity against a galloping Islamization."

Except there is no Judeo-Christian France versus anti-Semitic Muslims. In this ideological framing, France is often depicted as a unified static entity with one uniform common core from a cultural, linguistic, and religious standpoint when it has never existed that way. There is no "one" republic nor "one" essentialized French identity, especially not one centered on a supposed single Judeo-Christian heritage. Second, as Downing (2019) reminds us, from the Dreyfus Affair to the deportation of Jews during the Second World War, and the 74 percent increase in anti-Semitic incidents in France in 2018, France has strong and long roots of anti-Semitism. However, constructing a group, such as Muslims, as a discrete and homogeneous entity allows them to be essentialized into a single category possessing presumed essential characteristics used to predict behaviors labeled as dangerous. Downing (2019) explains that this framing process is called securitizing. Conceptualized by the Copenhagen School in the 1980s and 1990s, securitization first implies that the notion of security is not a mere objective fact but is an idea that is socially constructed in terms of the meanings, narratives, and thus policies attached to it. Second, the concept of securitization argues that assumptions about a group's homogeneity allow the dominant group to construct others as a security threat based on the violence of a few. Such assumptions support the clash of civilizations paradigm, which makes it seem that French and Muslims are on opposite and unreconcilable ends of the social values spectrum. However, this construction of French Muslims as a security threat isn't new. The production of stereotypical and prejudiced images of Muslims goes back to the colonial era: Muslim men and women have been Orientalized and exotified in terms of gendered roles in French popular culture, which has in turn been used to justify oppressive measures against them. The specific social construction of Muslims as a violent threat can be connected both to the colonial invasion and later the independence wars in North and West Africa, and to the idea of terrorist threats into the 21st century. Indeed, as examined in Chapter 5, during the 2005 ethnic riots, French Muslims in the *banlieues* were constructed by the French political class and by the media as a menacing, violent urban underclass. And they have more recently been represented as potential terrorists, based on presumed religiosity (and not social class), as demonstrated in the examination of President Macron's measures to fight "Islamist separatism." Thus, when in 2003 the then Minister of Interior Nicolas Sarkozy founded the French

Council of the Muslim Faith (Conseil Français du Culte Musulman), placed under the authority of the Minister of Interior, we should ask whether this was done in the spirit of openness or whether it represents yet another effort to control French Muslims.

The religion versus *laïcité* frame

On August 30, 2021, the French Minister of National Education launched a national communication campaign promoting *laïcité* in school that would last until September 2021, with eight different posters placed in the streets and as adverts on social media, as well as in schools. Per the Minister of Education's website, the campaign intended to show that the principle of *laïcité* is present in students' daily life, particularly their life at school, and that it "allows them to live free, [as] equals and united whatever their convictions." On the posters, middle and high school students of different races can be seen together in school activities (in classrooms, at the pool, or studying together). Their faces are visible, and the text printed over the images reads: "[G]iving the same course content to Romane, Elyjah and Alex, whatever their beliefs. That is what *laïcité* is." Or "Allowing Inès, Lenny, Simon and Ava to be together. That is what *laïcité* is." Another reads: "Allowing Sasha and Neissa to be in the same pool. That is what *laïcité* is." On each poster, we can see at least two children, at least one male student and one female student, and at least one White child and one child of color. From each image, along with the attached message, the implicit deduction when comparing names and genders is that a child with a presumed White Christian-sounding first name can be friends with a child of color (from their presumed nonWhite, non-Christian first name) thanks to the principle of *laïcité*. One of the implications of such images and messages is that students' races and possibly their religious beliefs are identified by proxies through their first names, which are implicitly linked to categorizing White people/Christians versus non-White people/ non-Christians, and thus, children of color are assumed to be non-Christians. The second implication is that the *laïcité* principle seems to be devaluing or minimizing the differences, and the diversity, portrayed by the students of color. As Tariq Modood (2012) claims, when examining whether secularism is experiencing a crisis in Western Europe, the main issue is about the perceived ethno-religious identities (for example Arab Muslim) in public life, and here most specifically in school settings. Such identities are linked to multiculturalism, which the French state sees as a challenge to its secularism and more largely to its constructed ideal of universalism.

The topic of Islam in France has long received attention from scholars and in popular culture given that the practice of religion in France is at the center of the French Republic and its republican ideal, more specifically, *laïcité*. In general, *laïcité* represents principles on the place of religion in French society.

At the legal level, *laïcité* is a constitutional principle separating church and state. The ideas behind the principle come from the 1789 French Revolution, and public education has been "laïc" or secular by law since 1882. But it is the law of 1905 that codifies the principles of *laïcité* in France: among other things, it confirms liberty of conscience (which was defended during the French Revolution) and the free exercise of religion. Although the law does not specify any particular religion, at the time the law was passed, lawmakers were mostly concerned with the protection of individuals from what they saw as undue religious pressures from the Catholic Church. The law also establishes the separation in that the French Republic will not recognize, fund, or pay salaries to any religious institution, with the exception of the departments of Alsace and Moselle, where religious leaders are paid and nominated by the local governments (the rationale being that the 1905 law was signed when Alsace–Moselle was German, not French). Additionally, the law prohibits the state and any of its representatives from giving any form of public support to particular religious beliefs. Finally, one of the implications of the law is that religious expression should be kept in the home and places of worship, and not in public schools. The reason is that after the French Revolution, the Catholic Church lost is right to teach its beliefs in the public educational system. And public schools became a place where children would learn to become citizens of the French Republic, through the teachings of moral and civics education. However, Downing (2019) explains that, on the one hand, the term *laïcité* only appears in the French Constitution during the Fourth Republic of 1946, despite the idea for it dating back to the 1789 French Revolution. On the other hand, Downing (2019) argues that *laïcité* itself does not have a formal legal definition other than the fact that it has a legal effect. Indeed, on the French government webpage dedicated to the notion of *laïcité*, it is simply presented in terms of its principles and attached values: the freedom of conscience and the liberty to express convictions; the separation of public institutions and religious organizations; and the equality of all before the law no matter their beliefs or convictions. In this sense, Downing (2019) claims that *laïcité* is a pillar of French national identity, even if it carries no legal definition. But even this description of the spirit of the notion of *laïcité* is both very specific and rather vague. Furthermore, the way the law enforces *laïcité* is done through different mechanisms and layers of application: for example, with regard to Islam, the burqa ban is enforced at the national level, the burkini ban at the regional level, and halal food provisions are enforced on a case by case basis in schools. Thus, the way that the principles of the law are applied differ according to the specific local institutions and contexts. As Downing (2019) explains, from the standpoint of the law, France is made up of layers of "multiple solitudes" and therefore multiple republics with diverse stakeholders and a multitude of state actors, agencies, and departments who all have different levels and styles of operationalization and engagement. The reality of how the law is operationalized stands in contrast with the first article of the French Constitution declaring that France is "one Republic indivisible." Such multiplicity of actors, levels, and solitudes also implies that the French state must constantly define exactly what *laïcité* means in context, and not just as a grand principle. Thus it requires constant interpretation and operationalization in order to function.

That being said, one significant aspect of the 1905 law that would have an impact on the issue of the headscarf affair discussed subsequently is that the law guarantees individuals the right to express any religious beliefs, provided these do not disturb the "ordre public" (public order). Among other things, this implies that individuals are not allowed to proselytize (that is, attempt to convince others to accept a particular religious opinion) in public spaces, including schools, though they are allowed to express their opinions in such places. And so, in effect, it followed that French middle or high school students were allowed to wear crucifixes, and neither wearing such religious insignia nor expressing religious views were prohibited.

The headscarf and burkini affairs

In 1989, what has come to be known as the "headscarf affair" erupted in France, and again in 1994, and again in 2003, until a 2004 law banned the garment from French public schools.

The controversy started in October 1989, when three Muslim girls, two of Moroccan and one of Tunisian origin, were expelled by their school in Creil, 30 miles north of Paris, because they were wearing headscarves. The director of the school, Mr. Chenière, found that their headscarf was in contradiction with the *laïcité* law. His decision to suspend the female students from school was brought to the attention of the media and the antiracist organization SOS Racisme, which appealed the decision to Lionel Jospin, the Minister of Education (under the presidency of Socialist François Mitterrand). Over the following months, the headscarf affair developed into a serious political controversy. Minister of Education Jospin sought advice from the Conseil d'Etat (State Council, the highest administrative court in France) on the matter and then decided to overturn Chenière's suspension order and to tolerate headscarves in state schools. Jospin's decision was met with strong opposition, including from leading French intellectuals like Régis Debray and Alain Finkielkraut, who compared the decision to "Munich," an expression referring to the 1938 Munich conference where Britain and France had submitted to the expansionist demands of Nazi Germany. This connection made by French intellectuals implied that the Islamic veil represented a comparable threat to the future of the French Republic. In fact, representatives of the right-wing party Rassemblement pour la République

(RPR, or Rally for the Republic) at the time, claimed that the headscarf was an act of provocation demonstrating the rejection of "shared values and principles of liberal individualism and secularism" (J0 25-10-1989 Lettinga and Saharso, 2012), and also as an act of self-segregation from the rest of society, also known as "repli communautaire" (withdraw into your own community), which is seen as dangerous to French integration.

Although the left and the right have a similar understanding of the universalist principles behind *laïcité* and religious neutrality in the public sphere, Socialists differed from the conservative party in their interpretation of the *laïcité* law. Minister of Education Jospin urged the students and their parents to "respect [the] principles of the state school, and not to come to school with any symbol that affirms a difference or religious distinction" (JO, 25-10-1989: 4113-4115). The Socialists believed that letting Muslim girls return to and attend school would help them integrate better into French society and emancipate them from their community's religious traditions.

Then in the fall of 1994, François Bayrou, the Minister of Education of the then center-right government, sent out a circular to all elementary and secondary school headteachers asking them to ban "ostentatious signs" of religious belief, which was connected with proselytism (*Le Monde*, September 21, 1994). In a press interview with the conservative magazine *Le Point*, Bayrou declared that he intended the ban to apply to headscarves but not to yarmulkas or crucifixes, which he classified as non-ostentatious (*Le Point*, September 10, 1994). However, the Conseil d'Etat ruled that there was no legal basis for declaring the wearing of the Islamic headscarf to be ostentatious or unlawful (*Le Monde*, July 12, 1995) and rendered Bayrou's circular null and void.

At the beginning of the 21st century, there had not been any increase in the number of girls wearing headscarves in state schools, and as a matter of fact, around 2003, it was at its lowest for many years (Hargreaves, 2007). And yet, in July 2003, French President Chirac (conservative party), who had previously supported a ban on the Islamic headscarf, set up a commission headed by friend and senior civil servant Bernard Stasi to review the specifics of the 1905 *laïcité* law, even though there was no particular urgency in the matter (as the number of headscarf-wearing student cases had declined). Nonetheless, in December 2003, the Stasi Commission published a report that included several recommendations, among which was a proposal to ban from state schools the wearing of religious insignia deemed to be ostentatious (Comité de Réflexion sur l'Application du Principe de Laïcité dans la République, 2004). At the same time, several members of the Socialist Party changed their perspective on the issue and decided to bring forth a legislative proposal to ban all religious, political, and philosophical symbols from school (no. 2096 in Lettinga and Saharso, 2012). Their rationale was that the headscarf is an expression of communitarianism, which is an obstacle to integration.

Shortly after the Stasi report's publication, President Chirac announced that legislation for a ban on religious symbols deemed too ostentatious would be rushed through the French Parliament. On March 15, 2004, the French government passed the law banning students from wearing conspicuous signs of religious affiliation in public schools. Chirac defined ostentatious – or conspicuous – as "those which lead to the wearer being immediately perceived and recognized by his or her religious affiliation." Some of the insignia to be banned included the Islamic veil (under whatever name), the yarmulka, and over-sized crosses. Other more "discreet" insignia such as a cross, the star of David, or the hand of Fatima are allowed. However, the law, and Chirac, did not give any specific definition or indication about the difference between a "manifestly over-sized" and a "discreet" insignia. In reality, the Stasi Commission had to perform some elaborate verbal acrobatics to justify the ban: a law could not solely ban the Islamic headscarf (which was the primary target) because it would have been rejected by the Conseil d'Etat as obviously discriminatory. And so, the law phrased the ban in more generally worded terms that included other religious insignia. Furthermore, interestingly, neither the Stasi Commission's report nor President Chirac gave any justification for how the wearing of such ostentatious insignia infringed the principle of laïcité.

However, by 2009, the French Parliament had started to debate the full face-cover or veil (or niqab). The debate originated with a decision by the Conseil d'Etat in June 2008 declaring that a Moroccan-born woman had been legitimately refused French citizenship because she was wearing a niqab, arguing that this showed an adherence to a "radical religious practice that conflicted with the values of the République," notably sex equality (no. 286798; Bertossi, 2012) On June 22, 2009, President Sarkozy declared in front of the Parliament: "The burqa is not a sign of religion, it is a sign of subservience. It will not be welcomed on the territory of the French Republic."

In August 2009, a woman wearing a burkini was prevented from entering a swimming pool. The decision was justified by a law preventing people from swimming in public pools with street clothes. However, despite the wish of Sarkozy to establish a law specifically banning public burqa-wearing, the Conseil d'Etat considered this possible law legally untenable. Thus, the government decided to launch a piece of legislation that would forbid all types of face-covering in all public spaces (including the street). At that point, the bill was framed in terms of maintaining social cohesion and public order, and in that regard, the face-veil could be considered an offense to the French republican social pact of living together. On June 13, 2010 at the National Assembly, a majority of 335 (right-wing and conservative representatives) voted in favor of the law, against 241 abstentions (most Socialist, Communist, and Green representatives). A majority in the Senate (246–1) also voted in favor of the government's legislation. Finally, the Constitutional Council declared that the law was in line with the French Constitution. More recently, in the summer of 2016, several mayors of cities in Southern France have deployed police forces to issue fines to women on public beaches, citing not wearing an "outfit respecting good morals and secularism" (*Le Parisien*, 2016).

On the one hand, despite the affirmation of Article 1 of the French Constitution that the French Republic "respects all the beliefs," the ban on the Islamic veil and the burkini is de jure and de facto about how the life of Muslim women should be structured under a secular republic. On the other hand, these battles mark the politicization and the framing of both garments as ethno-cultural differences in a debate where religion has become racialized.

The religion versus universalist feminism frame

In addition to arguments centered on the idea of the French Republic's cohesion through *laïcité*, the Islamic veil ban also used gender rights and supposed feminist arguments to gain support from the political and intellectual class. Indeed, as underlined by Jane Freedman (2007), one of the main arguments with regard to managing cultural differences in Western democracies is that granting group rights to minorities could be an impediment to advancing women's rights, which are defended through what are considered universal norms. So the wearing of the headscarf by young women at school is perceived in France as a sign of failure of the French republican system and model with regard to fully integrating second- and third-generation immigrants into French society (Freedman, 2007).

State Secretary for Gender Equality Issues Michèle André showed dissent and hesitation in defending the cabinet's tolerant stance toward the situation of the headscarf ban (JO, 8-11-1989: 4756-7). For her, the veil was a symbol of women's oppression and should have no place in school, a key institution for integration and emancipation. The defense of women's rights and gender rights as a central argument during the debates over the Islamic veil ban has been analyzed by Aurélien Mondon and Aaron Winter (2017b) as an imperialist, paternalistic, racist, and even sexist reassertion of the patriarchal order. Such gender rights arguments are rationalized into the supposed defense of women's emancipation from an oppressive (Muslim) patriarchal culture. But in fact, paradoxically, the Islam veil ban, which is supported by these universalist feminists, gives Muslim women the imperative to either remove their veil or pay a penalty, or remove themselves altogether from the public sphere and remain hidden in their private sphere. Such an imperative goes against feminist principles, which would instead demand more equal access to rights and resources for disenfranchised women. By supporting the Islamic veil ban, the supposedly universalist feminist frame reinforces the stigmatization of a gender and racial minority group of individuals without ever considering the agency of the person. As Christine Delphy (2006) shows, in the French debate over the hijab, many French feminists felt under pressure to make a false choice between racism and sexism. This is in part because women (who are not religious professionals) covering their body and face as part of their religious practice challenges the established norms of European feminism. And one of the consequences of the law itself is that Muslim women and girls are de jure excluded from public spaces, such as universities, swimming pools, public transport, and other places.

The rise of a universalist perspective against cultural relativism in French debates, particularly with regard to Islam, creates some tensions between mainstream feminists and multiculturalist feminists. We might view this as an irony, considering that feminists have long been critical of and challenged the universalizing definitions of gender. In France, this universalist egalitarian feminism is also rooted in secularism and has imposed itself as a universal homogenizing standard providing norms regarding women's emancipation. By supporting a headscarf ban, which thus imposes a hegemonic normative model (universalism), such secular feminists have denied Muslim women any form of agency. For example, French feminist Elisabeth Badinter, who defended the ban on the headscarf, believes that a secular universalism should be applied while denying women any possibility to be active agents capable of making their own choices. In a 2018 interview (*L'Express*, September 27, 2018), she also admits that the coming generation of women would be unable to accept the kind of feminism that she represents, because it is considered to be "too bourgeois, too 'white,' too inflexible on the question of universalism." In the same sentence, Badinter contradicts herself by advocating for universalism, which is presumably neutral and colorblind in her mind, while simultaneously recognizing that the racialized aspect of her "White" feminism is what would be problematic for new generations. Another French feminist, Caroline Fourest, also supports a secular republicanism and feminism and is critical of the cultural relativist approach. In particular, she has been very vocal against what she considers to be an Islamic threat. Fourest regularly attacks Islam and French Muslims in the French media, which has gained her recognition as being an expert on Islam, courageously defending the voice of universalism and feminism.

However, another French intellectual, philosopher Etienne Balibar, writes in French newspaper *Libération* (November 3, 1989) that the argument about the headscarf being a proof that women are oppressed by Islam is a frame that is used by Western societies to show their superiority over Muslim societies.

Yet, in their study assessing the effects of the French headscarf ban, Aala Abdelgadir and Vasiliki Fouka (2020) find that the ban had negative educational outcomes for the female students. Indeed, they find that the ban has disrupted women's educational trajectories and increased drop-out rates (due to school sanctions and expulsions) as well as the time taken to complete secondary education (with higher likelihood of repeating a class), and that it has also caused long-term disruption due to negative outcomes in terms of labor force participation and employment rates. Additionally, Abdelgadir and Fouka (2020) claim that the ban also altered the overall environment in schools and for the women attending the schools, where they lost support. In particular, through its application and the subsequent public debates over veiling, the law further stigmatized Muslims, especially with media discourses linking the headscarf to communitarianism and sexism perceived as opposed to the universalist feminist frame in France. Finally, Abdelgadir and Fouka (2020) argue, one effect of the headscarf ban may have been to cast the two identities of these female students (being French and Muslim) as incompatible, since the veil is de facto presented as a violation of French values and possibly a sign of inherent non-Frenchness. Other findings have shown that when excluded from a group due to perceived discrimination, individuals may withdraw and disengage from the discriminating majority. And yet, Abdelgadir and Fouka's study (2020) shows that women rejected the choice between their identities and reasserted themselves as both French and Muslim. As Beaman (2015, 2016) argues, this may of course be because they adapt their attitude and religious practice to gain acceptance in French society while trying to maintain their religious identity.

The religion and republican free speech frame

Another area in which a colorblind frame has been articulated concerns the question of the relationship between free speech and Islam, masked as a conflict between universalist republican principles and religion.

For example, in the aftermath of the terrorist attack against the satirical magazine *Charlie Hebdo* in Paris on January 7, 2015, the slogan "Je Suis Charlie" started to spread across France and the Western world, not only representing solidarity with the victims of the attack but also with what the magazine is thought to represent, namely the French republican and Enlightenment values of free speech. This widespread reaction of support was supposed to be in response to what is perceived as a threat posed by Muslim extremists and terrorists. However, as Mondon and Winter note (2017a), the events took place as Islamophobia was already significant in France following the debates around the headscarf affair. So the boundaries between a critique of extremism and terrorism, the defense of secular republican values, and Islamophobia have become blurry at best. And it is in that context that the "Je suis Charlie" slogan became somewhat of a movement, or at least a movement of thought, representing a civilizational project where France, and the Western world, stood as representatives of the values of free speech and secularism against what was presented as an attack by religion on the Republic's principles.

Hence the discussion centered on the imperative to uphold an absolute universal principle of freedom of speech against one specific threat, namely Islam, but presented as a question of a boundary between secularism and religion. For example, the justification given for publishing satirical cartoons mocking Islam was freedom of speech (which includes blasphemy). However, Roy et al (2006) claim that there seems to be a double standard in that no major newspaper would mock other groups in a similar way, more out of a fear of bad taste than of being sued for libel, and in this case it wouldn't be a matter of freedom of speech, but being able to satirize Islam and Muslims is presented as a symbolic rampart against intolerance and a defense of free speech for all. The unity behind the argument of freedom of speech comes from its colorblindness as it appeared as central to the French republican culture, identity, and democracy, and what it means to be French, which contradicts the idea of universalism. In that sense, Christophe Bertossi (2011) shows, using a national model like republican secularism to analyze and possibly justify a social and political phenomenon is in fact heavily normative. And we should be focusing on the assumptions about what is considered to be republican, how it was constructed, how it originated, and what it implies. But as Mondon and Winter (2017a) argue, such grand ideas have become mainstream and commonplace, and seem to have no historicity as well as being colorblind. This resulted in a shift of the subsequent debate after the *Charlie Hebdo* attack (and then even more after the terrorist attacks in Paris in November 2015 and Nice and Normandy in July 2016) from free speech versus religion to republican liberalism versus Islamophobia, where hardened positions against Islam by politicians and intellectuals seemed justified. In other words, colorblind arguments have allowed the justification of a colorblind racism with regard to Muslims and Islam in France, ensuring that the Muslim community was often presented as having foreign values and beliefs that were incompatible with French republicanism. In a 2015 interview (January 7, 2015), the former French Prime Minister, Mayor of Bordeaux, and runner-up in Les Républicains' primaries for the presidential elections declared after the *Charlier Hebdo* attack that it was the responsibility of French Muslims to speak up and defend an enlightened Islam. Similarly, French essayist and political commentator Eric Zemmour wrote in his 2014 book *The French Suicide*, which was widely publicized and popular (Mondon and Winter, 2017b), that the demise of France at the hands of Islam was the result of "the feminization and homosexualization of the country's population and politics, thus allowing a testosterone-fuelled and macho Muslim youth to take over." Finally, on January 6, 2016, the day before the first anniversary of the *Charlie*

Hebdo events, French feminist Badinter declared on France Inter radio that "one should not be scared to be called an Islamophobe."

Islam and secularism in Europe

In her study on the minaret ban in Switzerland, Jennifer E. Cheng (2015) notes that in Europe, Muslims are racialized according to the country where they reside: for example, in Britain, Muslims are racialized as South Asian people; in Germany, as Turkish people; in France, as people from the Maghreb; and in Switzerland, as Turkish people, Albanians, or Bosnians. Furthermore, Cheng (2015) argues, Muslim, as a religious identifier, can actually outweigh national identities, where people from the Maghreb or from Turkey may be perceived primarily as Muslim regardless of their actual religious affiliation, especially after 9/11.

One of the reasons Islam has been a topic of heated public debate in France and elsewhere in Europe is because it is framed by politicians as a measure of integration into mainstream society. In fact, Abdelgadir and Fouka (2020) argue, the policies used by European governments to regulate women's Islamic dress aim to achieve immigrant integration, preserve Western values, and reduce the visibility of a nonWhite religion in the public sphere.

However, studies show differences in the treatment of the Muslim populations in Europe: some countries have bans on headscarves (France, Germany, Russia), while others have laws specifically about the full-face veil (burqa or niqab) (Italy, Spain), and some countries have bans for both (France, Germany, the Netherlands), while other countries have no laws against headscarves (Sweden, the UK, Greece, Portugal, and others). Additionally, among the European countries where the ban is applied, it is done so by local governments differently depending on specific contexts, whereas the ban is applied in France by the government at the national level without any regard to specific situations. Nevertheless, a 2017 report (Howard, 2017) by the European Commission shows that even in countries that do not apply a ban on headscarves, legislative proposals may still have been put forward, and there may have been public debates on the question of the veil and/or the possibility of a ban. At the same time, the European Commission report (Howard, 2017) also indicates that several member states of the European Union have no legislation in place, no legislative proposal has been put forward, and no public debates about women wearing the veil have taken place: Cyprus, Estonia, Finland, Greece, Italy, Lithuania, Malta, Portugal, and Sweden are such examples.

In their study of the framing and regulations of headscarves in France, Germany, and the Netherlands, Doutje Lettinga and Sawitri Saharso (2014) compare the models of national citizenship in terms of their accommodating cultural differences to examine the impact on policies. France is identified as having a republican-secularist model promoting the idea of integration into French universal values for all its citizens. Germany follows an ethno-cultural corporatist model where the nation is conceived as a culturally homogeneous community with a common history, culture, and language. As a consequence, Germany only granted legal status as public corporations to the three main historical religious communities (Catholic, Evangelical, Jewish), and the Länder governments have refused to grant Islam the status of an officially recognized religion. Finally, the Netherlands is considered to be a multicultural pluralist model where the promotion of common values coexists with groups who have their own distinctive identities, and is thus open to the idea of cultural diversity.

Lettinga and Saharso (2014) have concluded that French society is the most restrictive in terms of policies regarding Islamic headscarves, while the Netherlands is the least restrictive, and Germany has some level of tolerance, albeit with restrictions at the local level. For example, Dutch society has accommodated its law on the veil to its Muslim population, compared with France, which has prohibited the Islamic veil in its many forms. France had a hesitant stance and tolerance of the headscarf in state schools, favoring a strict policy "limiting the space for difference" (Lettinga and Saharso, 2012), justifying this position with a universalist integration model. The Netherlands experienced a retreat from its multicultural integration model but not to the point of rejecting Islamic headscarves.

Furthermore, Claire Dwyer (1999: 5) notes that in the UK, Muslim women have been wearing the headscarf actively as part of what she calls the negotiation of difference, and "in the construction of their own identities both through challenging the meanings attached to different dress styles and in the reworking of meanings to produce alternative identities." However, Modood (2012) remarks, although Britain has no legislation against the veil, there seems to be popular support for a ban, even though none of the major political parties have put forward a legislative proposal.

Finally, with such a focus of the *laïcité* principle and law on the Islamic veil, as Meziane (2021: 125) notes in his study of systemic Islamophobia in France, "policing Islam tends to become ... the alpha and omega of state secularism itself."

In fact, according to Downing (2019), the securitization framing has taken over in France and in other European democracies. Muslims are often described as culturally alien and incapable of integration, particularly with the argument that the so-called multicultural project didn't work in Europe, when it was never really and thoughtfully implemented in the first place. As a result, Muslims are often viewed as a threat to the existence of Western liberal states and order. And framing them through the construction of security narratives and discourses provides ideological justification to implement racist policies.

Conclusion

Religion in France is a site of boundary construction. The role of the state in policing religion is not over, since the *laïcité* law of 1905, which demands a strict neutrality with regard to religion and religious practices, is a fundamental principle of the French Republic. At the same time, for centuries, Roman Catholicism has been the state religion in France – it has been institutionalized to the point that the recognition of major Christian holidays today is taken for granted in schools and the workplace in terms of schedules (Auslander, 2000). Furthermore, the display of nativity scenes in post offices and on public squares is not considered to violate the separation of church and state (Zolberg and Long, 1999). There is no equivalent recognition for Muslim holidays (Islam being the second religion in France, with 6 to 8 percent of the population identifying as Muslim in France, far behind the first religion, Catholicism, with an estimated 41 percent from the Eurobarometer survey of 2019). In a way, *laïcité* works to confine outsider religions to a marginal position rather than to one of parity in terms of treatment (Baubérot, 2000).

However, the absence of official data also leaves the narrative space open for politicians to use and exploit for political ends, enabling them to induce fear among the majority population by exaggerating numbers, knowing that Islamophobia has been growing throughout Europe and France for over a decade.

Laïcité can be thus analyzed as a form of fantasized neutrality, which is really a form of indirect and covert yet active state management of religion, where instead of guaranteeing freedom of belief, as expressed in the law, religious practice is heavily regulated and controlled, but only for Muslims. Additionally, this chapter showed a paradox in the rationalization of French republican principles: *laïcité* is supposed to be the grand and grounding principle of the French Republic, a sort of neutral space based on secularism, beyond the influence of a state religion. And yet, French politicians often refer to the Judeo-Christian tradition to which France fundamentally belongs. One of the reasons is that Christianity is not seen as a threat to the foundations of the French Republic because it is associated with White French culture, whereas Islam is framed as dangerous to the French Republic because of its connection to immigration from former colonies in North Africa. According to Cheng (2015), this perception of the threat posed by Islam is pervasive in France, and in much of Europe more broadly, due to the fact that Islam is conflated with a nonWhite religion, and as such, its practices and values are perceived not only as contrary to White French (White European) values and norms but also as a potential threat to a liberal-democratic country. Furthermore, Islam is also seen, by White Europeans, as a threat because it is perceived as increasingly influential on the political and legal order in France and other European countries. In fact, depicting Muslims as a monolithic group through essentialization supports the image of a unified community threatening the state and the dominant social order.

As shown in the case of the headscarf and burkini affairs, Islam and its visible signs are framed as incompatible not only with the essence of French law but with the essence of the French Republic in its supposed neutrality and what it means to be truly French. Except that the justification for the headscarf ban is grounded in a colorblind narrative, based on the defense of the rule of law about liberal equality and rights (freedom of speech, gender rights) supposedly associated with the origins of the French Republic. This colorblind explanation can be analyzed as a clear example of colorblind racism, using the pretense of secularism to target Muslim communities in France (Tevanian, 2005; Scott, 2007). Therefore, although the laws of 2004 and 2011 banning the hijab and the burqa impose a significant stigma on certain practices, which actually tend to essentialize and equate Muslims with Arab people, they are not seen as overtly racist policies because of the focus on *laïcité*. And research actually challenges the discourse that universal rights will necessarily benefit women's status and advancement in society, especially Muslim women (Freedman, 2007). In fact, Abdelgadir and Fouka (2020) note, not only has the headscarf ban had negative effects on the women affected by it, at least in terms of educational outcomes, but it has also proven unhelpful in integrating them into French society. Similarly, Freedman (2007) notes that imposing laws specifically on certain groups of women (Muslims) does not improve the position of all women, but rather only reinforces state power over groups that are already experiencing prejudice and discrimination.

Thus, using Bonilla-Silva's colorblind racism theoretical framework, this chapter has argued that the way supporters of the laws have framed the issues of the Islamic veil, or the response to the *Charlie Hebdo* terrorist attack, is by defending a republican universalist ideal that can be declined through various repertoires. In this case, the repertoires that act as dominant racial frames providing an intellectual road map for colorblind racism are *laïcité*, gender rights, and freedom of speech. For example, secular feminism is also based on a constructed universalist ideal that contradicts a multicultural non-essentialist approach of feminism. In any case, they are all variations of republican secularism and universalism, both ideologies used to justify the exclusion of and discrimination against Muslims, as well as the racialization of religion, particularly Islam and Christianity, to delineate what it means to be French. What such a frame provides is to racialize an element of social status without having to use the term race or racial categories. That is precisely what a colorblind society does. And yet, by doing so, the state reinforces colorblind racism. Also, the systemic marginalization of Muslims in France is often presented in terms of religious exclusion or discrimination, when it is also connected to race and class status (Downing, 2019). And indeed, the bans show that the French government is in fact tasking the courts with deciding what is considered appropriate in terms of racial difference and assimilation.

As Bertossi (2020) explains, the invention of a supposed colorblind or neutral French tradition emanating from the French Revolution and the Enlightenment, and what he calls the "crystallization of this historical repertoire," have allowed for the emergence of key principles such as integration, communitarianism, and *laïcité*. These principles have in turn helped define "traditional national values and ideologies" (Lamont, 1992: 136). As a result of this ideological framing, Muslims have been constructed as the least valued members of French society (Bertossi, 2020).

This form of colorblind racism uses frameworks and language from the French Enlightenment to support racist ideologies, making it what I term an "enlightened racism."

Rethinking Integration and Racial Identity: Beyond the French Exception

A post-racial world?

In 2008, the simple fact that Obama was elected president was interpreted as solid evidence that such a victory of diversity in the highest political institution of the United States would "automatically yield race-neutral practices" (Ostertag and Armaline, 2011). At the time, this idea of a post-racial society was applauded by the French media and political elite. However, in contrast to popular claims that Obama's election and presidency is an indicator that we have moved on to become post-racial societies where race and racism have become irrelevant, many scholars have demonstrated that systemic racism has persisted and evolved into a largely covert system that draws strength from its ability to be elusive (Ostertag and Armaline, 2011). As suggested by race scholars like Feagin and Bonilla-Silva, contemporary racism has "shape shifted" (Neubeck and Cazenave, 2001) into colorblind racism, a central ideological component of this new racism that emerged in the post-civil rights era.

In the context of France, this book has shown that the dominant ideological framework of colorblindness, prevailing in a post-racial world and postcolonial society, is very much part of a "white racial hegemony" (Neubeck and Cazenave, 2001) that helps contemporary racism endure in a more covert way, from which it gets its strength. And because policies (employment, housing, education, police) appear colorblind, they have remained largely unchallenged and unquestioned by the French political elite, even if they are called into question by social justice movements and organizations.

However, as this book has demonstrated, colorblind narrative assertions seem unrealistic and problematic because they are not only delusional when confronted with the recurring realities of systemic racism but because they also participate in the persistence of a colorblind racism by supporting a White racial framing of the issue.

Biologists have established that racial categories among humans do not exist, in the sense that there are no homogeneous human groups with intrinsic characteristics entirely different from and unequal to others that would define them as completely separate, biologically speaking, from other human groups. And although skin color has been used historically to distinguish human groups, it is only one marker among many others of geographic and historical affiliation. As French social scientist Magali Bessone (2013b: 71) asserts: "[T]here is no racial essence that can be defined coherently from a biological point of view." Yet, as social scientists (Lewis, 2004; Bonilla-Silva, 2006; Golash-Boza, 2016) have demonstrated, while race isn't biologically relevant, it is nonetheless socially significant. Other research scientists have shown the salience of race and racial categories more specifically in French society, from the 15th century to the contemporary context (Peabody, 1994; De Rudder, 1996; Bleich, 2000; Peabody, 2004; Fassin, 2006; Tobner, 2007; Fassin and Simon, 2008; Beaman, 2019; Beaman and Petts, 2020; Beaman, 2021).

Despite the elimination of the word race from the French Constitution in July 2018, the current French Penal Code, the 1948 United Nations Universal Declaration of Human Rights, the 1966 International Pact on Civil and Political Rights, the 1950 European Convention of Human Rights, and the European Chart of Fundamental Rights proclaimed in Lisbon in 2007 all include many direct references to the word race. Furthermore, the constitutions of several European countries – Germany, Italy, Spain, and so on – contain the word race. Thus at first glance, France's proclaimed colorblindness sounds like a cultural and societal exception, not only in Europe but in many other parts of the world, including Africa, Asia, North America, and South America.

However, through a review of sociological scholarship on race, this book has analyzed the contradictions and paradoxes that exist in French scholarship and current public policies with regard to the treatment of racial diversity in France, and more specifically with regard to French racial minorities. It has done so by focusing its analysis on significant issues in contemporary French society: the debates on ethnic statistics, the 2005 French riots, the persisting patterns of racial discrimination, and the contentious public policies toward the Islamic veil, which all point to the central issues of colorblindness and systemic racism. Additionally, by applying American theoretical frameworks in sociology (such as colorblind racism and the White racial frame) to the French context, this book has sought to offer an alternative analysis to the understanding of the singularity of the French context in Europe with regard to its treatment of racial diversity and systemic racism.

Chapter summary

Chapter 2 in troduced and defined the terms central to the analysis of this book, namely race and racism. It also reviewed the history of race in France, including the links between race and colonialism, as well as slavery. Additionally, it presented the main theoretical frames relevant to the study of race and racial diversity as they apply to this particular case-study, notably the works of Joe Feagin and Eduardo Bonilla-Silva, but also Jennifer C. Mueller. Chapter 2 also exposed the main contradictions, and questions, rising from past and current debates among French scholars and political actors with regard to race and racism in France.

Chapter 3 examined the paradoxes of the French model of integration, which is based on the republican ideal of universalism but in fact perpetuates and maintains the structures of institutional racism in contemporary France, whether for immigrants, children of immigrants, and more particularly for French racial minorities. In particular, this chapter exposed the problematic effects of colorblindness and of the French government's current reforms and policies that use a culturalized narrative (or ethnicity) as a proxy for race, which still has consequences in the 21st century, notably with regard to discrimination patterns against racial minorities in sectors like employment, education, housing, health, and police profiling and brutality.

Chapter 4 analyzed the structure of the French census and other state-sanctioned enumeration processes in France and explored the relationship between France's colorblind discourse with regard to racial categorization and the material conditions of racial inequality. The chapter also offered an alternative to previous explanations of why France refuses to include race and ethnicity in its census. This chapter also considered sociological research on comparative case studies in Europe, examining the way other countries classify, adopt, deny, or negotiate racial categories.

Chapter 5 described the 2005 French riots that took place in the French *banlieues*. It reviewed the current literature that has examined the riots and provided an analysis of the riots as they pertain to the larger question of racial identity. Finally, it demonstrated the 2005 riots' significance in the larger context of the discursive and institutional structure that is the French model with regard to racial identity.

Chapter 6 exposed the problematic narrative and racial framing linked to the promotion of *laïcité*, of a universalist feminism, and of the principle of republican freedom of speech in France, which all tend to racialize Islam and perpetuate discrimination against French Muslims, particularly women.

Main findings

Although France and the United States have profoundly different histories and contexts (and are yet intimately related), French society has nonetheless been marked by slavery, colonization, and immigration. And although France has long perceived the notions of ethnicity and race as imports imposed from the United States, this book has brought forth evidence that the idea of race, and racial categorization, has in fact been present within the legal and ideological frameworks of French society since at least the 16th century. Second, this book has also demonstrated that the refusal to acknowledge and take into account the existence of race as a marker of inequality in the treatment of minority populations comes from a denial at the state level. This denial is at the source of what this book identifies as colorblind racism. The wish to pretend that race is not there emanates in part from centuries of oppression and exploitation of people of color and the unsaid desire to hide the colonial past and avoid responsibility for it. Denial is also a way to avoid interrogating the present policies of discrimination and structural racism plaguing French society.

For Denys Cuche (2008), the root causes of the tendency for the French social sciences to lag behind on this issue are both ideological and epistemological. For Patrick Simon (2008a), the collective blindness and silence among French institutions is a choice of ignorance.

Throughout this book, it has been my contention that ignoring and rejecting the notion of race, and preventing social scientists from collecting data on race and ethnicity, means precluding the understanding of one of the fundamental forms and forces of social stratification in contemporary France, and as a result failing to grasp some of the most important mechanisms that produce and maintain inequality.

The question of taking race into account has political, ideological, legal, epistemological, and methodological ramifications, but it is also about providing the ability to see and hear the experience of many individuals and groups with regard to discrimination and racism. Continuing to disregard the existence of everyday practices will not eliminate them.

This book offers four main findings.

First, the French case-study is a life-size illustration of what it means to be a colorblind society and what it means for a colorblind society to operate. It is a case-study for all those who argue that the answer to eliminating racism is to eliminate race: indeed, France doesn't acknowledge race in its census or otherwise and yet, racism, racial discrimination, and racial segregation, persist and flourish. Despite, and even with the help of, colorblind policies and structures, racism is maintained and supported in France thanks to the many levels of denial and ignorance. And so, the larger implication of this study is to show, in fact, that colorblindness is not the solution to eliminating racism but rather reinforces it, hidden in plain sight. Through the study of the French case, not only do we learn that colorblindness at the state level (through institutions and structures) is not the answer to racism, but it may also help us to think about, discuss, and imagine a global theory of race and racism that does not involve pretending races don't exist.

Second, this book has shown that despite all appearances of colorblindness, there is a contradiction in terms: French official institutions deny the existence of race, eliminate it from all official documents, including the highest one (the French Constitution), and yet Whiteness is at the core of French national identity, and people of color in France are constantly reminded of that fact (in the workplace, by the police). In fact, as argued by Beaman (2018), Whiteness is at the core of many national identities. Therein lies the contradiction: the French republican ideal may deny the existence of race, and also hide the significance of racism, but by emphasizing through many forms of exclusion, segregation, and discrimination that racial minorities cannot be completely French because they are not White, it also makes Whiteness the norm in terms of belonging. It does not erase Whiteness or make it invisible – quite the contrary, it makes it the standard in plain sight, making it seem the "neutral" point of reference, and in this sense, colorblind.

Third, through the examination of the French census, as well as specific issues such as discrimination laws and patterns in France, the 2005 ethnic riots, and the place of Islam in France, this book has unveiled the mechanisms of colorblindness, and particularly what I call the grammar of colorblind racism, based on different strategies and repertoires.

Drawing on the theoretical frameworks of American sociologists Feagin (White racial frame), Bonilla-Silva (colorblind racism), and Mueller (racial ignorance), this book has uncovered the strategies and repertoires used by different institutions of French society that help maintain the illusion of colorblindness, thus reinforcing colorblind racism itself.

As seen throughout the chapters, colorblind strategies include:

- the denial that race exists as a central structuring component of French social life;
- the refusal to use racial categories in the French census, despite strong support from French sociologists and demographers to do so in order to collect accurate data;
- the use of proxies or euphemisms in lieu of racial and ethnic terms that actually point to the reification of the notion of national identity meaning that the French government treats national identity as a cultural object marking an idea of "us versus them", but without the acknowledgment of racial diversity within French national identity;
- the minimization or denial of the role ethnicity or race play in discrimination patterns and instead claiming other nonracial factors (socioeconomic) may cause it;
- a reluctance to design institutions and policies focusing on race even while fighting systemic racism.

All these strategies support the overall mechanism of White ignorance. Indeed, ignoring race allows for several outcomes: it avoids referring to the wrongdoings of France's past colonial regimes; it avoids recognizing the existence of racial minority groups in France, some of whom are from former colonies; it avoids engaging in a national discussion, and most importantly reckoning, that systemic racism is present and thriving in France and needs to be addressed at the political and socioeconomic levels.

The repertoires that provide nonracial justifications for the current colorblind social order in contemporary France include:

- French Republicanism, resting on the French Revolution normative principles of "Liberty, Equality, Fraternity," is the gatekeeper to citizenship, and implicitly frames French citizens as white but presents citizenship as a neutral notion, while framing non-white individuals as outsiders, who are potentially perceived as threats to the Republican order.
- Abstract French universalism and its ideals, which, despite its contradiction in terms, are also expressed through the French Republican ideology coming from the French Revolution and the Enlightenment philosophy, considers that some universal principles govern French society and are seen as incompatible with race-conscious approaches like multiculturalism, or communautarism, which pay attention to otherness, differences, and cultural relativism, notably in terms of race.
- Laïcité, and its principles regarding the separation of church and state, which emanates from the secular Republican ideals of the French Revolution, has become a moral framework that defines French identity, masking a discourse about racial and ethnic differences, and has served as a frame of reference to evaluate issues such as the Islamic headscarf, but also freedom of speech and gender rights with regards to religion.

All these repertoires help sustain the French model of integration, which entails a philosophy, a policy paradigm, and an institutional and discursive opportunity structure. More specifically, the repertoires also provide colorblind explanations and justifications to French social order and to social injustices created within and by that social order. All are attempts at erasing the notion of race as a central structuring element to social life, and at minimizing both race and racism to explain socio-economico-political inequalities and injustices at the micro, meso, and macro levels in French society.

Bonilla-Silva (2006) explains that the central component of any dominant racial ideology is its frames or set paths for interpreting information. In some ways, the form of colorblind racism examined in the French case uses frameworks and language from the French Enlightenment to support racist ideologies, which, I contend, makes it an "enlightened racism."

First, what I call enlightened racism relies on fantasized ideals of the French Revolution and the Enlightenment, one that presents philosophers from the 18th century as champions of the values of liberty, equality, and fraternity for all citizens when, in fact, renowned thinkers like Montesquieu and Voltaire put forward elaborate theories about the enslavement of Africans, while Rousseau simply ignored it. Second, an enlightened racism also makes the claim that the ideals and principles that emerged from the French Revolution – republicanism, universalism, *laïcité* – are neutral in their essence, and based on intellectually sound arguments that are only here to serve all French citizens, outside of racial considerations. As such, an enlightened colorblind racist ideology is in fact producing White racial ignorance instead, committed to ignore and deny the principle of social reality that includes enduring racial hierarchies and inequalities. Third, an enlightened racism is not based on bigotry, or a lack of education, or a personal phobia. Rather, it is based on an intellectually elaborate frame of argument that uses Enlightenment philosophical principles as a normative discourse and narrative to interpret reality. In turn, this normative discourse is used as an explanation either to defend personal racist attitudes or to justify racist institutional policies.

Fourth, this book also questioned the notion of integration or assimilation models and their normative assumptions. As Bertossi (2011) notes, often, the problem with using national integration models to evaluate the success of immigrants and racial minorities is that they are biased and ill-founded, because they are elite-shaped frames that have been reified without questioning. For example, the French republican model is still seen as an ideal type with notions, like *laïcité*, that have not been deconstructed, but rather idealized, and have also become normative, even though they are colorblind. And as Bertossi (2011) explains, the paradox is that we tend to link and correlate models (which are seldom defined) of integration or assimilation to an empirical reality and to the success of the model itself, as a standard for policymaking. But often, we don't know how useful the models are as analytical tools. Bertossi (2011: 6) says that we can't simply point out the contradictions of the model while continuing to accept "an imagined normative republic."

Conclusion

The point of this book was to question and unmask the French model of integration in terms of its approach to race, and its normative assumptions, and to give it a sense of historicity. This model of integration or assimilation is based on a colorblind (no race) and religious blind (*laïcité*) citizenship that presumably incorporates differences into Frenchhood, but without recognizing those differences. The French model of integration presumably leading to equality rests on the idea of nonrecognition of racial differences and diversity. But in fact, this model of citizenship cannot predict the success or failure of institutions and structures that are designed as colorblind when the reality isn't. In fact, the colorblindness of the French republican model is masking a brutal reality of daily segregation, discrimination, and overall racism, as lived by racial minority groups whose experience is denied by a colorblind system. Many racial minorities in France experience not just a double bind but a triple one, with an accumulation of social, territorial, and racial factors multiplying their effect when added together to produce significant negative consequences, sometimes even lethal, directly or indirectly, short term and long term. A fourth additional harm comes from the colorblind system and ideology that is prevalent in France within the structures and institutions, preventing any recognition of issues that are in fact deeply rooted in racial inequalities and injustices, and thus directly related to race.

Thus, for a radical transformation to take place in the French context aiming to promote racial diversity, equity, and justice, there is first a need to evaluate accurately the patterns of racial discrimination, segregation, and systemic racism that is experienced not only by immigrants but also by French racial minorities. And for that to happen, as Magali Bessone (2013b) argues, first and foremost there needs to be an acknowledgment of the existence of race. Systemic racism is not just a question of resources and material production; it is also about the construction of ideologies justifying the racial order, where unequal access to resources is the norm. Because, in fact, with regard to the notion of race, French society has many levels of denial in the form of White ignorance (Mueller, 2020): denial that race is a central structuring element of social life; denial that race has actually been at the heart of French history for centuries; denial that race is at the center of debates and policies hiding itself under the masks of universalism, laïcité, or republicanism; and denial that race is in fact used every day in daily interactions, on school playgrounds, or in intellectual circles. As underlined by Beaman and Petts (2020), French society may officially present itself as colorblind at the macro or state level, and as such, could be perceived as an exception among other European nations, but it is not blind at the micro or everyday level. Both Keaton (2013) and Fassin and Fassin (2006) similarly claim that France's ethos is simultaneously constructed as colorblind and color conscious. Beaman (2021: p 2) further argues that "France is both anti-racial in that the French reject the use of racial terms, and nonracial, in that it denies the reality of race." In some ways, in French society, race is very much present everywhere but recognized nowhere. But France isn't colorblind: as shown earlier in this book, race has been historically central to the construction of French identity. And it is not that race disappeared and is reappearing today. It was a denegation, not a disappearance. France willfully ignores that it is a racialized society. It has intentionally placed race in its blind spot. And it is this intentional ignorance of race that allows racism to persist and White privilege to be reproduced and maintained as a hegemonic ideology in contemporary France.

Finally, if the French state wishes to make progress and headway in realizing racial diversity within its institutions (politics, schools, universities, public and private sectors), it needs to "make ignorance hard" (Mueller, 2017: 235) and raise race-consciousness, by actively recognizing the salience of race in contemporary French society. This process may require the creation of racial or ethnic categories, and thus allowing social scientists to collect racial data in order to uncover and understand the mechanisms of the existing racial hierarchy and of White supremacy.

The fabric of French society throughout history and in contemporary France is racial diversity. Simply turning a blind eye to race and pretending it doesn't exist, or pretending it has no significance, will not make race or racism go away.

Policy recommendations

Finally, I would like to conclude this book by proposing a set of policy recommendations, as they have been suggested by different scholars (Jung and Donnard, 2016; Beaman, 2021), that could help address some of the current lacunae of the French system with regard to race-consciousness. Indeed, not being able to collect racial or ethnic statistics prevents social scientists from reflecting the existing racial diversity, but also the current socioeconomic disparities and inequalities in France.

- Allow the French state census to collect ethnic/racial statistics.
- Allow research scientists, under university regulations and review, to collect ethnic/racial statistics.
- Include race in the studies on police brutality and police violence (for example racial profiling).
- Develop networks of social actors (politicians, social scientists, political activists, nongovernmental organizations) to elaborate collectively a reflection around the question of racial discrimination and diversity in French society.
- Include discussions about racial discrimination in the initial training and continuing education of health professionals, allowing them to interrogate their own representations, and train them to know the legal framework, to identify possible discriminatory situations, and build relevant and appropriate responses.
- Develop a reflection that includes the different concerned social actors about the means and methods to use to improve spatial fluidity in terms

of access to housing (rent or ownership) in order to fight residential segregation and racial discrimination in housing.

- Mobilize the leadership at public institutions – schools, hospitals, social services – around the issues related to the effective equity of services that are provided, and the issues of discrimination in the treatment of individual cases (for example patient care).
- Set up spaces of reflection within public institutions to build regulations on discrimination and diversity issues, as well as put in place alert protocols for situations of discrimination.
- Propose antidiscrimination policies that specifically and clearly include race.
- Examine a way to enforce and use more efficiently existing tools in public institutions allowing for a real equity in access to rights.
- Reinforce an interinstitutional vigilance system through durable mechanisms to avoid risks of racial discrimination during transition of leadership.
- Broadcast antidiscrimination laws on race to the public more efficiently for a better knowledge and use of recourse in case of discrimination, so that citizens have easy access to the legal framework regarding racial discrimination.
- Provide, reinforce, make accessible free legal support for individuals bringing discrimination cases to court of justice.
- Recognize the place of racial minorities in French political and social life.
- Promote better representation of racial minorities in public institutions, including government.
- Demand that France acknowledges its role in colonialism and discuss reparations with former colonies, going beyond the report ordered by President Macron, and written by French historian Benjamin Stora (2021), regarding the role of France in the colonization of Algeria, which does not explicitly discuss nor demand that France recognizes its crimes, apologizes, or gives reparations.
- Include a more extensive and significant place to the study of France's history of colonialism in education programs at the middle and high school levels.

Glossary

Color line the expression the "problem of the color line" refers to a sentence written by American sociologist W.E.B. DuBois in his 1903 book, *The Souls of Black Folk*. In his book, DuBois argues that the problem of the twentieth century will be the "problem of the color line", the implication being that the differences and inequalities in socio-economic and political status between Whites and Blacks in 20th century United States would be prevalent and significant.

Descendant of DOM (overseas department of France) native-born person born in metropolitan France with at least one parent born in a DOM.

Descendant of immigrants person residing in France, born in metropolitan France with a least one immigrant parent.

Foreigner person residing in France without French citizenship.

Immigrant person residing in France, born abroad with a foreign nationality at birth, but who could have acquired French citizenship while in France. This definition excludes French citizens born abroad (children of expatriates, former colonizers).

DOM native-born person born in one of the French overseas departments.

Mainstream population persons who are not immigrants or descendants of one or more immigrants, or who are not DOM native-born, or descendants of one or more DOM native-born person. Most of the mainstream population is born in metropolitan France with two parents born in metropolitan France, but the group also includes French citizens born abroad (repatriates from the former French colonies or children of expatriates).

INSEE   Institut National de la Statistique et des Etudes Economiques, or National Institute of Statistics and Economic Studies is a Directorate-General part of the French Ministry of the Economy and Finance. Its mission is to collect, analyze, and disseminate information on the French demography, economy, and society across the entire French territory.

INED   Institut National d'Etudes Démographiques, or French Institute for Demographic Studies. A public research institute specializing in population studies that works with academic and research communities at the national and international levels.

CNIL   Commission Nationale de l'informatique et des Libertés, or National Commission on Informatics and Liberty. An independent administrative authority whose mission is to ensure that the data privacy law (French Law of 1978) is applied to the collection, storage, and use of personal data.

TeO   Trajectoires et Origines, or Trajectories and Origins, a population survey on diversity in France conducted between 2008 and 2009, where about 22,000 individuals born between 1948 and 1990 were interviewed. The survey was organized jointly by INED and INSEE.

ZFU   Zones Franches Urbaines, or Urban Tax-free Zones, urban areas of more than 10,000 inhabitants that are classified by French government as tax-free, where companies can set up and are exempted from tax and social security contributions for five years. The criteria taken into consideration to be declared a ZFU are:

- the unemployment rate;
- the percentage of people in the population without any degree or diploma;
- the percentage of youth; and
- the fiscal potential per inhabitant.

ZUS   Zones Urbaines Sensibles, or Sensitive Urban Zones, urban areas considered by French government as high-priority targets for public policies and funding because of their disadvantaged socioeconomic status. There are 751 ZUS in France.

The Law no. 78-17 of January 6, 1978, called Informatics and Freedoms Law (Loi Informatique et libertés), relative to informatics, data, and freedoms, constitutes the foundation of protection of personal data in terms of data treatment on French territory. It regulates the freedom of treatment of personal data. The 1978 law was amended with a law of August 6, 2004, which transposed the European directive of October 24, 1995 on the protection of personal data. The 2004 law reduces the obligation for the owners of data files to declare anything, it increases the power of the CNIL with regard to direct in-person controls and sanctions, and it reinforces the rights of individuals. The law also creates a group of "correspondants" (Correspondants Informatique et Libertés, CIL), professionals who are in charge within their organization (company, administration, local government) to ensure that the 1978 law is respected.

References

Abdelgadir, Aala and Vasiliki Fouka. 2020. Political secularism and Muslim integration in the West: assessing the effects of the French headscarf ban. *American Political Science Review*, 114(3): 707–23.

Athari, Elika, Yaël Brinbaum, and Jérôme Lê. 2019. Le role des origines dans la persistance des inégalités d'emploi et de salaire. *Insee Références: Dossier Emploi, Chômage, Revenus du Travail*, Edition 2019: 29–46.

Aubry, Bernard and Michèle Tribalat. 2009. Les jeunes d'origine étrangère. *Commentaire*, 126: 431–7.

Auslander, Leora. 2000. Bavarian crucifixes and French headscarves: religious signs and the postmodern European State. *Cultural Dynamics*, 12(3): 283–309.

Azria, Elie, Priscille Sauvegrain, Julie Blanc, Catherine Crenn-Hebert, Jeanne Fresson, Maud Gelly et al. 2020. Racisme systémique et inégalités de santé, une urgence sanitaire et sociétale révélée par la pandémie COVID-19: pour la commission Inégalités sociales et parcours de soins du Collège National des Gynécologues Obstétriciens Français CNGOF. *Gynecologie, Obstetrique, Fertilite & Senologie*, 48(12): 847–49.

Badiou, Alain. 2005. L'humiliation ordinaire. *Le Monde*, November 15. Available from: http://www.lemonde.fr/idees/article/2005/11/15/l-humi liation-ordinaire-par-alainbadiou_ 710389_3232.html [Accessed February 27, 2015].

Balibar, Etienne. 2007. Uprising in the *banlieues*. *Constellations*, 14: 47–71.

Baubérot, Jean. 2000. *Histoire de la laïcité française*. Paris: PUF Collection.

Barthes, Roland. 1970. L'ancienne rhétorique: aide-mémoire. *Communications, Recherches Rhétoriques*, 16: 172–223.

Bauer, Alain. 2006. *Fichiers de police et de gendarmerie: comment améliorer leur contrôle et leur gestion*. La Documentation Française.

Beaman, Jean. 2015. Boundaries of Frenchness: cultural citizenship and France's middle-class North African second-generation. *Identities*, 22(1): 36–52.

Beaman, Jean. 2016. As French as anyone else: Islam and the North African second generation in France. *International Migration Review*, 50(1): 41–69.

Beaman, Jean. 2017. *Citizen Outsider: Children of North African Immigrants in France*. Oakland: University of California Press.

Beaman, Jean. 2018. Black versus European: Frantz Fanon and the over-determination of Blackness. In Marcus Anthony Hunter (ed) *The New Black Sociologists: Historical and Contemporary Perspectives*, New York: Routledge, pp 42–8.

Beaman, Jean. 2019. Are French people white? Towards an understanding of whiteness in republican France. *Identities*, 26(5): 546–62.

Beaman, Jean. 2021. Race: a never-ending taboo in France. *Georgetown Journal of International Affairs*, April.

Beaman, Jean and Amy Petts. 2020. Towards a global theory of colorblindness: comparing colorblind racial ideology in France and the United States. *Sociology Compass*, 14(4) (April): 1–11.

Beauchemin, Cris, Christelle Hamel, Maud Lesné, Patrick Simon, and l'équipe de l'enquête TeO. 2010. Les discriminations: une question de minorités visibles. *Populations et Sociétés*, 466: 1–4.

Bébéar, Claude. 2004. Des entreprises aux couleurs de la France. *La Documentation française*. Available from: https://www.institutmontaigne.org/publications/des-entreprises-aux-couleurs-de-la-france [Accessed August 9, 2022].

Benbassa, Esther. 2005. Un appel controversé contre le racisme 'anti-blancs'. *Le Nouvel Observateur*. 31 March.

Bereni, Laure. 2009. Faire de la diversité une richesse pour l'entreprise: la transformation d'une contrainte juridique en catégorie managériale. *Raisons Politiques*, 35: 87–106.

Bereni, Laure and Vincent-Arnaud Chappe. 2011. La discrimination, de la qualification juridique à l'outil sociologique. *Politix*, 94(2): 7–34.

Berger, Peter L. 1969. *The Sacred Canopy: Elements of a Sociological Theory of Religion*. New York: Anchor Books.

Bertossi, Christophe. 2011. National models of integration in Europe: a comparative and critical analysis. *American Behavioral Scientist*, 55(12): 1561–80.

Bertossi, Christophe. 2012. The performativity of colour blindness: race, politics and immigrant integration in France, 1980–2012. *Patterns of Prejudice*, 46(5): 427–44.

Bertossi, Christophe. 2016. *La citoyenneté à la Française*. Valeurs et Réalités. Paris: CNRS.

Bertossi, Christophe. 2020. Uses of history as a cultural process: integration, citizenship and the boundary-making in contemporary France. *Journal of Ethnic and Migration Studies*, 47(18): 4238–55.

Bertrand, Marianne and Sendhil Mullainathan. 2005. Are Emily and Greg more employable than Lakisha and Jamal? A field experiment on labor market discrimination. *American Economic Review*, 94(4): 991–1013.

Bessone, Magali. 2013a. Racial or spatial categorisations? A focus on the French setting. *Theoria*, 137(60): 48–67.

Bessone, Magali. 2013b. *Sans distinction de race? Une analyse critique du concept de race et de ses effets pratiques.* Paris: Vrin, Philosophie concrète.

Bessone, Magali. 2017. Racisme, justice, respect. *France Culture*, January 30.

Billaud, Julie and Göle Nilüfer. 2011. Islamic difference and the return of feminist universalism. In Anna Tryandifillidou, Tariq Modood, and Nasar Meer (eds) *European Multiculturalisms: Cultural, Religious and Ethnic Challenges*, Edinburgh: Edinburgh University Press, pp 116–41.

Blanchard, Emmanuel. 2014. Contrôles au faciès: une cérémonie de dégradation. *Plein Droit*, 103(4): 11–15.

Blanchard, Emmanuel. 2018. La colonialité des polices françaises.In Jérémie Gauthier and Fabien Jobard (eds) *Police: Questions sensibles*, Paris: Le Seuil, pp 37–50.

Bleich, Erik. 2000. Antiracism without races: politics and policy in a colorblind state. *French Politics, Culture, & Society*, 18(3): 48–74.

Bleich, Erik. 2001. The French model: colorblind integration. In John David Skrentny (ed) *Color Lines: Affirmative Action, Immigration, and Civil Rights Options for America*, Chicago: University of Chicago Press, pp 270–96.

Bleich, Erik. 2003. *Race Politics in Britain and France: Ideas and Policymaking since the 1960s.* Cambridge: Cambridge University Press.

Bleich, Erik. 2011. What is Islamophobia and how much is there? Theorizing and measuring and emerging comparative concept. *American Behavioral Scientist*, 55(12): 1581–600.

Bleich, Erik, Carolina Caeiro, and Sarah Luehrman. 2010. State responses to "ethnic riots" in liberal democracies: evidence from Western Europe. *European Political Science Review*, 2(2): 269–95.

Bonelli, Laurent. 2005. Les raisons d'une colère. *Le Monde Diplomatique*, December. Available from: http://www.monde-diplomatique.fr/2005/12/BONELLI/12993 [Accessed February 27, 2015].

Bonilla-Silva, Eduardo. 2006. *Racism without Racists: Colorblind Racism and the Persistence of Racial Inequality in the United States.* Lanham: Rowman & Littlefield.

Bonilla-Silva, Eduardo. 2014. *Racism without Racists: Colorblind Racism and the Persistence of Racial Inequality in the United States. Fourth Edition.* Lanham: Rowman & Littlefield.

Bonnet, François and Clothilde Caillault. 2015. The invader, the enemy within and they-who-must-not-be-named: how police talk about minorities in Italy, the Netherlands and France. *Ethnic and Racial Studies*, 38(7): 1185–201.

Bonnet, François, Etienne Lalé, Mirna Safi, and Etienne Wasmer. 2015. Better residential than ethnic discrimination! *Sciences Po/Laboratoire interdisciplinaire d'évaluation des politiques publiques*, 5 (September): 1–8.

Borrillo, Daniel. 2003. *Lutter contre les discriminations.* Paris: La Découverte.

Boulainvilliers, Henri de. 1727. *Histoire de l'ancien gouvernement de la France*. The Hague: Aux dépens de la Compagnie.

Bourdieu, Pierre. 1979. *La distinction: Critique sociale du jugement*. Paris: Les Editions de Minuit.

Bourdieu, Pierre and Loïc Wacquant. 1999. On the cunning of imperialist reason. *Theory, Culture, and Society*, 16(1): 41–58.

Brinbaum, Yaël, Laure Moguérou, and Jean-Luc Primon. 2012. Les enfants d'immigrés ont des parcours scolaires différenciés selon leur origine migratoire: immigrés et descendants d'immigrés en France. *INSEE Références*.

Brut. 2020. Emmanuel Macron répond à Brut. December 4. Available from: https://www.elysee.fr/emmanuel-macron/2020/12/04/le-presid ent-emmanuel-macron-repond-aux-questions-de-brut [Accessed April 14, 2022].

Byrd, W. Carson. 2011. Conflating apples and oranges: understanding modern forms of racism. *Sociology Compass* 5(11): 1005–17.

Calvès, Gwénaële. 2000. Les politiques françaises de lutte contre le racisme, des politiques ne mutation. *French Politics, Culture & Society*, 18(3): 75–82.

Calvès, Gwénaële. 2004. *La discrimination positive*. Paris: PUF.

Campbell, Karlyn Kohrs. 2005. Agency: promiscuous and protean. *Communication and Critical/Cultural Studies*, 2(1): 1–19.

Carde, Estelle. 2007. Les discriminations selon l'origine dans l'accès aux soins. *Santé Publique*, 19(2): 99–109.

Carde, Estelle. 2011. De l'origine à la santé, quand l'ethnique et la race croisent la classe. *Revue européenne des migrations internationales*, 27(3): 31–55.

Carrère d'Encausse, Hélène. 2005. 'Beaucoup de ces Africains sont polygames ...'. *Libération*, 15 November.

Castel, Robert. 2007. *La discrimination négative: citoyens ou indigènes*. Paris: Editions du Seuil et la République des Idées.

Cavanagh, Allison and Alex Dennis. 2012. Behind the news: framing the riots. *Capital and Class*, 36(3): 375–81.

Césaire, Aimé. 1939, 1956. *Cahier d'un retour au pays natal*. Paris: Présence Africaine.

Chapman, Herrick and Laura L. Frader (eds). 2004. *Race in France: Interdisciplinary Perspectives on the Politics of Difference*. New York: Berghahn Books.

Cheng, Jennifer C. 2015. Islamophobia, Muslimophobia or racism? Parliamentary discourses on Islam and Muslims in debates on the minaret ban in Switzerland. *Discourse and Society*, 26(5): 562–86.

Cognet, Marguerite. 2020. Les services de santé: lieu d'un racisme méconnu. In Omar Slaouti (ed) *Racismes de France*, Paris: La Découverte, pp 74–86.

Cuche, Denys. 2008. Roger Bastide, le "fait individuel" et l'école de Chicago. *Cahiers Internationaux de sociologie*, 1(124): 41–59.

D'Appolonia, A.C. 2009. Race, racism and anti-discrimination in France. In Sylvain Brouard, Andrew M. Appleton, and Amy Gale Mazur (eds) *The French Fifth Republic at Fifty: Beyond Stereotypes*. London: Palgrave Macmillan, pp 267–85.

Défenseur des Droits. nd. Lutte contre les discriminations et promotion de l'égalité. Available from: https://www.defenseurdesdroits.fr/fr/institution/competences/lutte-contre-discriminations [Accessed August 5, 2022].

Défenseur des Droits. nd. Antidiscriminations. Available from: https://www.antidiscriminations.fr/ [Accessed August 5, 2022].

Delpeuch, Thierry, Jacqueline E. Ross, and François Bonnet. 2017. Les analyses sociologiques des relations police-population: vers une reconnaissance de la variété des pratiques policières; présentation du dossier. *Droit et Société*, 97(3): 457–68.

Delphy, Christine. 2006. Antisexisme ou antiracisme? Un faux dilemme. *Nouvelles Questions Féministes*, 26(1): 59–83.

DeLuca, Kevin Michael. 1999. *Image Politics: The New Rhetoric of Environmental Activism*. New York: Guilford Press.

Demiati, Nasser. 2007. Nicolas Sarkozy, ministre de l'Intérieur et pompier pyromane. In L. Mucchielli and V. Le Goaziou (eds) *Quand les banlieues brûlent … Retour sur les émeutes de Novembre 2005*. Paris: Editions La Découverte, pp 58–77.

De Rudder, Véronique. 1996. Race. In Pierre-Jean Simon (ed) *Vocabulaire historique et critique des relations inter-ethniques*. Paris: L'Harmattan, pp 111–13.

De Rudder, Véronique and François Vourc'h. 2006. Les discriminations racistes dans le monde du travail. In Didier Fassin and Eric Fassin (eds) *De la question sociale à la question raciale: représenter la société française*, Paris: Editions La Découverte, pp 183–99.

Dhume, Fabrice. 2013. La sociologie de la discrimination ethnique à l'école, éléments d'une histoire française. In *Diversité-Ville-Ecole-Intégration, La ville, l'école, la diversité: quarante ans de solidarité*, 174: 135–41.

Donnet, Claire, Mélanie Fraisse, Nicolas Horvat, Ananda Melo-King, and Johanna Probst. 2010. Des processus de "racisation". *Raison*, 174: 39–51.

Downing, Joseph. 2019. *French Muslims in Perspective: Nationalism, Post-Colonialism and Marginalisation under the Republic*. Basingstoke: Palgrave Macmillan.

Duguet Emmanuel, Noam Leandri, Pascale Petit and Yannick l'Horty. 2010. Are young French jobseekers of ethnic immigrant origin discriminated against? A controlled experiment in the Paris Area. *Annals of Economics and Statistics*, 99-100: 187–216.

Duprez, Dominique and Harlan Koff. 2009. The 2005 riots in France: the international impact of domestic violence. *Journal of Ethnic and Migration Studies*, 35(5): 713–30.

Dussieux, Louis. 1873. *Géographie Générale: la géographie physique, politique, administrative, historique, agricole, industrielle et commerciale de chaque pays*. Paris: Librairie Jacques Lecoffre.

Dwyer, Claire. 1999. Veiled meanings: young British Muslim women and the negotiation of difference. *Gender, Place and Culture*, 6(1): 5–26.

Eberhardt, Jennifer L., Phillip A. Goff, Valerie J. Purdie, and Paul G. Davies. 2004. Seeing black: race, crime, and visual processing. *Journal of Personality and Social Psychology*, 87: 876–93.

Erdenir, Burak. 2010. Islamophobia qua racial discrimination. In Anna Triandafyllidou (ed) *Muslims in 21st Century Europe: Structural and Cultural Perspectives*, London: Routledge, pp 27–44.

Escafré-Dublet, Angéline, and Patrick Simon. 2014. Une citoyenneté controversée: descendants d'immigrés et imaginaire national. In Marie Poinsot (ed) *Migrations et mutations de la société française: l'état des savoirs*, Paris: La Découverte, pp 248–56.

Escafré-Dublet, Angéline, Lionel Kesztenbaum, and Patrick Simon. 2020. When French Muslims were counted in the census. *Population & Societies*, 583(11): 1–4.

Education Ministère. nd. Lancement d'une campagne nationale de promotion de la laïcité à l'école. Available from: https://www.education.gouv.fr/lancement-d-une-campagne-nationale-de-promotion-de-la-laicite-l-ecole-324737. [Accessed April 14, 2022].

European Commission. 2019. Report on discrimination in the European Union. Special Eurobarometer 493.

Fanon, Frantz. 1967. *Black Skin, White Masks*. New York: Grove Press.

Farkas, Lilla. 2017. Analysis and comparative review of equality data collection practices in the European Union: data collection in the field of ethnicity. Luxembourg: Publications Office of the European Union.

Fassin, Didier. 2002. L'invention française de la discrimination. *Revue française de science politique* 52(4): 403–23.

Fassin, Didier. 2006. Nommer, interpréter: le sens commun de la question raciale. In Didier Fassin and Eric Fassin (eds) *De la question sociale à la question raciale?*, Paris: Editions La Découverte, pp 27–44.

Fassin, Didier. 2011. *La Force de l'Ordre*. Paris: Le Seuil.

Fassin, Eric. 2006. Aveugles à la race ou au racisme? Une approche stratégique. In Didier Fassin and Eric Fassin (eds) *De la Question Sociale à la Question Raciale? Représenter la Société Française*, Paris: Editions La Découverte, pp 114–38.

Fassin, Didier and Eric Fassin. 2006. Conclusion: éloge de la complexité. In *De la Question Sociale à la Question Raciale? Représenter la Société Française*, Paris: Editions La Découverte, pp 249–59.

Fassin, Didier and Patrick Simon. 2008. Un objet sans nom: introduction des discriminations raciales dans la statistique française. *L'Homme*, 187–8: 271–94.

Feagin, Joe R. 2009. *The White Racial Frame: Centuries of Racial Framing and Counter-Framing*. New York: Routledge.

Feagin, Joe R. 2010a. *Racist America. Roots, Current Realities, and Future Reparations*. New York: Routledge.

Feagin, Joe R. 2010b. *The White Racial Frame. Centuries of Racial Framing and Counter-Framing*. New York: Routledge.

Feagin, Joe R. 2012. *White Party, White Government: Race, Class and U.S. Politics*. New York: Routledge.

Feagin, Joe R. and Adia H. Wingfield. 2013. *Yes We Can? White Racial Framing and the Obama Presidency*. New York: Routledge.

Felouzis, Georges, Barbara Fouquet-Chauprade, and Samuel Charmillot. 2015. Les descendants d'immigrés à l'école en France: entre discontinuité culturelle et discrimination systémique. *Revue française de pédagogie*, 191: 11–27.

Ferrand, Olivier. 2012. L'axe UMPFN: vers le parti patriote? *Synthèse Terra Nova*, June 12.

Finchelstein, Gilles. 2011. La stratégie du pyromane. *Notes de la Fondation Jean-Jaurès*, 85: 1–3.

Fleming, Crystal. 2017. *Resurrecting Slavery: Racial Legacies and White Supremacy in France*. Philadelphia: Temple University Press.

Foucault, Michel. 1984. The order of discourse. In Michael J. Shapiro (ed) *Language and Politics*, New York: New York University Press, pp 108–38.

Freedman, Jane. 2007. Women, Islam and rights in Europe: beyond a universalist/culturalist dichotomy. *Review of International Studies*, 33: 29–44.

Gaillard, Jean-Michel. 1995. *L'ENA, miroir de l'etat: de 1945 à nos jours*. Paris: Complexe.

Gardell, Mattias. 2014. Crusader dreams: Oslo 22/7, Islamophobia, and the quest for a monocultural Europe. *Terrorism and Political Violence* 26(1): 129–55.

Garfinkel, Harold. 1956. Conditions of successful degradation ceremonies. *American Journal of Sociology*, 61(5): 420–4.

Gèze, François. 2006. Les "intégristes de la République" et les émeutes de novembre ou les effets de la mutation médiatique de la figure de l'intellectuel. *Mouvements* 44: 88–100.

Gillespie, Andra. 2009. Obama, race and Henry Louis Gates. *Politico*, 23 July. Available at http://www.politico.com/news/stories/0709/25329.html [Accessed July 28 2022].

Golash-Boza, Tanya. 2015. *Race and Racisms: A Critical Approach*. New York: Oxford University Press.

Golash-Boza, Tanya. 2016. A critical and comprehensive sociological theory of race and racism. *Sociology of Race and Ethnicity*, 2(2): 129–41.

Gray, Doris H. 2008. *Muslim Women on the Move: Moroccan Women and the French Women of Moroccan Origin Speak Out*. Plymouth: Lexington Books.

Göle, Nilüfer and Julie Billaud. 2011. Islamic difference and the return of feminist universalism. In Modood, Tariq, Anne Triandafyllidou, and Nasar Meer (eds) *European Multiculturalisms: Cultural, Religious and Ethnic Challenges*. Edinburgh University Press, pp 116–41.

Hall, Stuart. 1993. Encoding, decoding. In Simon During (ed) *The Cultural Studies Reader*, London: Routledge, pp 98–102.

Hargreaves, Alec G. 1995. *Immigration, "Race" and Ethnicity in Contemporary France*. London: Routledge.

Hargreaves, Alec G. 2005. An emperor with no clothes? Social Science Research Council, November 28.

Hargreaves, Alec G. 2007. *Multi-Ethnic France: Immigration, Politics, Culture and Society*. New York: Routledge.

Héran, François. 2005. France/Etats-Unis: deux visions de la statistique des origines et des minorités ethniques. *Santé, Société et Solidarité* 1: 167–89.

Herrnstein, Richard J. and Charles Murray. 1994. *The Bell Curve: Intelligence and Class Structure in American Life*. Free Press.

Hollinger, David A. 2008. Obama, the instability of color lines, and the promise of a post-ethnic future. *Callaloo*, 31(4): 1033–4.

Hollinger, David A. 2011. The concept of post-racial: how its easy dismissal obscures important questions. *Daedalus*, 140(1): 174–82.

Howard, Erica. 2017. Religious clothing and symbols in employment: a legal analysis of the situation in the EU member states. European Commission, Directorate-General for Justice and Consumers, Brussels.

Hunt, Darnell M. (1997) *Screening the Los Angeles "Riots": Race, Seeing, and Resistance*. Cambridge: Cambridge University Press.

INSEE. 2016. Insee en bref: pour comprendre la mesure des populations étrangère et immigrée. April.

INSEE. 2020. France, portrait Social. Immigrés et descendants d'immigrés.

INSEE. 2021a. Décomposition de la population vivant en France selon le lieu de naissance et la nationalité. Données Annuelles de 2006 à 2020. Available from: https://www.insee.fr/fr/statistiques/2865118 [Accessed August 9, 2022].

INSEE. 2021b. L'essentiel sur … les immigrés et les étrangers.

Jobard, Fabien and Omar Slaouti. 2020. Police, justice, etat: discriminations raciales. In Omar Slaouti and Olivier Le Cour Grandmaison (eds) *Racismes de France*, Paris: La Découverte, pp 41–58.

Jung, Emily and Gaëlle Donnard. 2016. Discriminations dans le champ de la santé: les repérer et les prévenir tout au long du parcours de soins. Migrations santé Alsace/ORIV – Note de synthèse – Groupe de travail "Santé et discriminations." Jugnot, Stéphane. 2007. Statistiques raciales. *Libération*, 2 October.

Kateb, Kamel. 2004. La statistique coloniale en Algérie (1830–1962): entre la reproduction du système métropolitain et les impératifs d'adaptation à la réalité algérienne. *Courrier des Statistiques* 112: 3–17.

Keaton, Trica Danielle. 2013. Racial profiling and the French exception. *French Cultural Studies*, 24(2): 231–42.

Kokoreff, Michel. 2009. Ghettos et marginalité urbaine. *Revue française de sociologie*, 50(3): 553–72.

Lagrange, Hugues. 2006. Autopsie d'une vague d'émeutes. In Hugues Lagrange and Marco Oberti (eds) *Emeutes Urbaines et Protestations: Une singularité française*, Paris: Presses de la Fondation Nationale des Sciences Politiques, pp 37–58.

Lagrange, Hugues and Marco Oberti (eds). 2006. *Emeutes urbaines et protestations: une singularité française*. Paris: Presses de la Fondation Nationale des Sciences Politiques.

Lamont, Michele. 1992. *Money, Morals, and Manners: The Culture of the French and American Upper-Middle Class*. Chicago: Université of Chicago Press.

Lang, Kevin and Jee-Yeon K. Lehmann. 2012. Racial discrimination in the labor market: theory and empirics. *Journal of Economic Literature*, 50(4): 959–1006.

Leblanc, Damien. 2019. Les Sauvages: une fresque politique audacieuse et amère. *Première*. 20 September. Available from: https://www. premiere.fr/Series/News-Series/Les-Sauvages-une-fresque-politique-audacieuse-et-amere--critique [Accessed August 9 2022].

Le Parisien. 2016. Le Conseil d'Etat suspend l'arrêté anti-burkini sur les plages de Villeneuve-Loubet. August 26.

Lettinga, Doutje and Sawitri Saharso. 2012. The political debates on the veil in France and the Netherlands: reflecting national integration models? *Comparative European Politics*, 10(3): 319–36.

Lettinga, Doutje and Sawitri Saharso. 2014. Outsiders within: framing and regulations of headscarves in France, Germany and the Netherlands. *Social Inclusion*, 2(3): 29–39.

Lewis, Amanda. 2004. "What group?" Studying whites and whiteness in the era of color-blindness. *Sociological Theory*, 22(4): 623–46.

Lochak, Danièle. 1987. Réflexions sur la notion de discrimination. *Droit Social*, 11: 778.

Lochak, Danièle. 2003. Loi du marché et discrimination. In Daniel Borrillo (ed) *Lutter contre les discriminations*, Paris: La Découverte, pp 9–37.

Love, Bettina L. and Brandelyn Tosolt. 2010. Reality or rhetoric? Barack Obama and post-racial America. *Race, Gender & Class*, 17(3–4): 19–37.

Macé, Eric. 2005. Banlieues: des territoires abandonnés? *Le Monde*, November 7. Available from: http://www.lemonde.fr/societe/chat/2005/11/04/banlieues-des-territoires-abandonnes-chat-realise-le-7-novembre-2005_706489_3224.html [Accessed February 27, 2015].

Marlière, Eric. 2011. Émeutes urbaines, sentiments d'injustice, mobilisations associatives. *Sociologies, Théories et recherches*, July 6. Available from: http://sociologies.revues.org/3521 [Accessed February 27, 2015].

Masclet, Olivier. 2009. *Sociologie de la diversité et des discriminations*. Armand Colin Collection 128.

Masclet, Olivier. 2017. *Sociologie de la diversité et des discriminations*. Paris: Armand Colin.

Matas, Juan and Roland Pfefferkorn. 2010. Le problème de la ligne de partage des couleurs. *Raison Présente: Racisme, race, et sciences sociales*, 174: 3–12.

Maurin, Eric. 2004, *Le ghetto français: enquête sur le séparatisme social*. Paris: Le Seuil (La république des idées).

McAvay, Haley. 2017. The ethnoracial context of residential mobility in France: Neighborhood out-migration and relocation. *Population Space Place*, 24: 21–38.

McAvay, Haley. 2018. The ethnoracial context of residential mobility in France: neighborhood out-migration and relocation. *Population, Space and Place*, 24(6).

Merklen, Denis. 2006. Paroles de pierre, images de feu: sur les événements de novembre 2005. *Mouvements*, 43: 131–7.

Merle, Pierre. 2012. À qui profitent les dépenses éducatives? *La vie des idées*, May 22. Available from: https://laviedesidees.fr/A-qui-profitent-les-depenses.html#:~:text=Le%20sociologue%20Pierre%20Merle%20dresse,%C3%A9laboration%20de%20toute%20r%C3%A9forme%20%C3%A9ducative [Accessed April 14, 2022].

Messer, Chris M. and Patricia A. Bell. 2010. Mass media and governmental framing of riots: the case of Tulsa, 1921. *Journal of Black Studies*, 40(5): 851–70.

Meurs, Dominique. 2017. The role of discrimination in immigrant unemployment. *Population & Societies*, 546: 1–4.

Meziane, Mohamad Amer. 2021. Introduction: on police violence and systemic Islamophobia. *Political Theology*, 22(2): 125–9.

Modood, Tariq. 2012. Is there a crisis of secularism in Western Europe? *Sociology of Religion*, 73(2): 130–49.

Mondon, Aurélien. 2015. The French secular hypocrisy: the extreme right, the Republic and the battle for hegemony. *Patterns of Prejudice*, 49(4): 392–413.

Mondon, Aurélien. 2016. Defending the indefensible: France, the burkini affair and the further mainstreaming of racism. Open Democracy. Available from: https://www.opendemocracy.net/en/can-europe-make-it/defending-indefensible-france-burkini-affair-and-further-mainstre/ [Accessed July 28 2022].

Mondon, Aurélien and Aaron Winter. 2017a. Charlie Hebdo, republican secularism and Islamophobia. In Gavan Titley, Des Freedman, Gholam Khiabany, and Aurélien Mondon (eds) *After Charlie Hebdo: Terror, Racism and Free Speech*, London: ZED Books, pp 31–45.

Mondon, Aurélien and Aaron Winter. 2017b. Articulations of Islamophobia: from the extreme to the mainstream. *Ethnic and Racial Studies*, 40(13), 2151–79.

Monso, Olivier and Thibaut de Saint Pol. 2007. Geographic origin of individuals in French population censuses. *Courrier des statistiques, English series* 13: 51–60.

Moran, Matthew. 2008. Challenging the Republic: interpreting the 2005 urban violence in French suburbs. *Opticon1826* (4): 1–7.

Moran, Matthew. 2011. *The Republic and the Riots: Exploring Urban Violence in French Suburbs, 2005–2007*. Oxford: Peter Lang.

Mucchielli, Laurent. 2009. Autumn 2005: a review of the most important riot in the history of French contemporary society. *Journal of Ethnic and Migration Studies*, 35(5): 731–51.

Mucchielli, Laurent and Véronique Le Goaziou (eds). 2007. *Quand les Banlieues Brûlent ... Retour sur les Émeutes de novembre 2005*. Paris: Editions La Découverte.

Mueller, Jennifer C. 2017. Producing colorblindness: everyday mechanisms of white ignorance. *Social Problems*, 64: 219–38.

Mueller, Jennifer C. 2020. Racial ideology or racial ignorance? An alternative theory of racial cognition. *Sociological Theory*, 38(2): 142–69.

Murray, Graham. 2006. France: the riots and the Republic. *Race & Class*, 47(4): 26–45.

Ndiaye, Pap. 2006. Questions de couleur: histoire, idéologie et pratiques du colorisme. In Didier Fassin and Eric Fassin (eds) *De la question sociale à la question raciale?*. Paris: Editions La Découverte, pp 45–52.

Neubeck, Kenneth and Noel A. Cazenave. 2001. *Welfare Racism: Playing the Race Card against America's Poor*. New York: Routledge.

Noiriel, Gérard. 2007a. *Immigration, Antisémitisme et Racisme en France (XIXe–XXe siècle): Discours Publics, Humiliations Privées*. Paris: Fayard.

Noiriel, Gerard. 2007b. Le nationalisme "soft" de Nicolas Sarkozy. *Mouvements*, March 29.

Noiriel, Gérard. 2008. Constructions et usages de l'identité nationale. In *Conference at Université Populaire de Gennevilliers* [podcast]. January 15. Available from: http://www.intempestive.net/spip.php?article15 [Accessed February 27, 2015].

Observatoire des Inégalités. 2005. Qu'est-ce que la discrimination positive? *Propositions*, July 6.

Observatoire des Inégalités. 2021. *Des contrôles de police très inégaux selon la couleur de peau.* March 11.

Observatoire des Inégalités. 2022. Définir et mesurer les discriminations. *Notes de l'Observatoire, No. 7.* May.

Oreopoulos, Philip. 2011. Why do skilled immigrants struggle in the labor market? A field experiment with thirteen thousand resumés. *American Economic Journal: Economic Policy*, 3(4): 148–71.

Ostertag, Stephen F. and William T. Armaline. 2011. Image isn't everything: contemporary systemic racism and antiracism in the age of Obama. *Humanity & Society*, 35(3): 261–89.

Palczewski, Catherine H., Richard Ice, and John Fritch. 2012. *Rhetoric in Civic Life.* State College: Strata Publishing.

Palomares, Elise. 2013. Racism: a blind spot in French urban sociology? *Metropolitics*, October 2.

Pan Ké Shon, Jean-Louis. 2009. L'émergence du sentiment d'insécurité en quartiers défavorisés: dépassement du seuil de tolérance ... aux étrangers ou à la misère? *Espace, Populations, Sociétés* 1: 105–17.

Pan Ké Shon, Jean-Louis. 2010. The ambivalent nature of ethnic segregation in France's disadvantaged neighborhoods. *Urban Studies*, 47(8): 1603–23.

Pan Ké Shon, Jean-Louis. 2011. Residential segregation of immigrants in France: an overview. *Populations & Sociétés*, 477 (April).

Pan Ké Shon, Jean-Louis and Claire Scodellaro. 2011. Discrimination au logement et ségrégation ethno-raciale en France. *Documents de Travail*, INED, 171.

Pan Ké Shon, Jean-Louis and Claire Scodellaro. 2018. The living environment of immigrants and their descendants: perceived discrimination and segregation. In Cris Beauchemin, Christelle Hamel, and Patrick Simon (eds) *Trajectories and Origins: Survey on the Diversity of the French Population*, Cham: Springer, pp 143–70.

Peabody, Sue. 1994. Race, slavery, and the law in early modern France. *The Historian*, 56(3): 501–10.

Peabody, Sue. 2004. "A nation born to slavery": missionaries and racial discourse in seventeenth-century French Antilles. *Journal of Social History*, 38(1): 113–26.

Peabody, Sue and Tyler Stovall (eds). 2003. *The Color of Liberty: Histories of Race in France.* Durham: Duke University Press.

Père du Tertre. 1654. *Histoire Générale des Isles de St Christophe, de la Guadeloupe*. Paris: Hachette, BNF.

Piketty, Thomas and Mathieu Valdenaire. 2006. L'impact de la taille des classes sur la réussite scolaire dans les écoles, collèges et lycées français. *Les Dossiers*, 173. Ministère de l'Education Nationale.

Poggioli, Sylvia. 2009a. 'Obama effect' instills hope in Europe's minorities. *NPR*. January 12. Available from: https://www.npr.org/templates/story/story.php?storyId=99247328 [Accessed August 9 2022].

Poggioli, Sylvia. 2009b. French minorities push for equality post-Obama. *NPR*. January 14. Available from: https://www.npr.org/templates/story/story.php?storyId=99298290 [Accessed August 9 2022].

Riach, Peter A. and Judith Rich. 2002. Field experiments of discrimination in the market place. *Economic Journal*, 112(483): 480–518.

Rigouste, Mathieu. 2011. *L'ennemi intérieur: La généalogie coloniale et militaire de l'ordre sécuritaire dans la France contemporaine*. Paris: La Découverte.

Rivenbark, Joshua G. and Mathieu Ichou. 2020. Discrimination in healthcare as a barrier to care: experiences of socially disadvantaged populations in France from a nationally representative survey. *BMC Public Health*, 20(31): 1–10.

Roberts, Dorothy. 2012. *Fatal Invention: How Science, Politics, and Big Business Re-create Race in the Twenty-first Century*. New York: New Press.

Roché, Sebastian. 2006. *Le Frisson de l'émeute: violences urbaines et banlieues*. Paris: Editions du Seuil.

Roy, Olivier. 2005. The nature of the French riots. Social Science Research Council, November 18.Roy, Olivier, A. Bidar, and O. Mongin. 2006. Les caricatures de Mahomet. *Esprit*, 3: 323–35.

Saada, Emmanuelle. 2014. Et le droit colonial inventa l'indigène. *L'Histoire*, 400(June).

Sabbagh, Daniel and Shanny Peer. 2008. French color blindness in perspective: the controversy over "statistiques ethniques". *French Politics, Culture & Society*, 26(1): 1–6.

Sall, Rouguyata. 2019. Observatoire de la laïcité: des religions plus visibles, mais des fidèles moins nombreux. Médiapart, July 11.

Sayad, Abdelmalek. 1999. *La double absence: des illusions de l'émigré aux souffrances de l'immigré*. Paris: Éd. du Seuil.

Sayegh, Pascal-Yan. 2008. Discursive elements in the (de)banalization of nationalism: a study of speeches by Gordon Brown and Nicolas Sarkozy. CFE Working Paper Series, 35: 1–26.

Schneider, Cathy L. 2008. Police power and race riots in Paris. *Politics & Society*, 36(1): 133–59.

Scott, Joan Wallach. 2007. *The Politics of the Veil*. Princeton: Princeton University Press.

Silverman, Maxim. 1992. *Deconstructing the Nation: Immigration, Racism and Citizenship in Modern France*. London: Routledge.

Simiti, Marilena. 2012. The volatility of urban riots. In Seraphim Seferiades and Hank Johnston (eds) *Violent Protest, Contentious Politics, and the Neoliberal State*, Farnham: Ashgate, pp 133–45.

Simon, Patrick. 2003. L'impasse de l'analyse statistique dans une France sans "races". *Hommes et Migrations*, 1245: 42–53.

Simon, Patrick. 2008a. The choice of ignorance: the debate on ethnic and racial statistics in France. *French Politics, Culture & Society* 26(1): 7–31.

Simon, Patrick. 2008b. Les statistiques, les sciences sociales françaises et les rapports sociaux ethniques et de "race". *Revue Française de Sociologie* 49(1): 153–62.

Simon, Patrick. 2012. *French National Identity and Integration: Who Belongs to the National Community?* Migration Policy Institute.

Simon, Patrick. 2014. Available from: https://www.INED.fr/en/everythi ng_about_population/demographic-facts-sheets/researchers-words/patr ick-simon [Accessed April 14, 2022].

Simon, Patrick. 2017. The failure of the importation of ethno-racial statistics in Europe: debates and controversies. *Ethnic and Racial Studies*, 40(13): 2326–32.

Simon, Patrick. 2020. L'invisibilité des minorités dans les chiffres du coronavirus: le détour par la Seine-Saint Denis. In Solène Brun and Patrick Simon (eds) *Dossier, Inégalités ethno-raciales et pandémie de coronavirus*, Institut des Migrations, Aubervilliers: De Facto.

Simon, Patrick and Joan Stavo-Debauge. 2004. Les politiques anti-discrimination et les statistiques: paramètres d'une incohérence. *Sociétés Contemporaines* 53: 57–84.

Simon, Patrick and Mirna Safi. 2013. Les discriminations ethniques et raciales dans l'enquête Trajectoires et Origines : représentations, expériences subjectives et situations vécues. *Economie et Statistique*, 464–6.

Smith, Dorothy E. 1993. The standard North American family: SNAF as an ideological code. *Journal of Family Issues*, 14(1): 50–65.

Smithson, Michael. 2008. Social theories of ignorance. In R.N Proctor and L. Schiebinger (eds) *Agnotology*. Stanford: Stanford University Press, pp 209–29.

Stolz, Jörg. 2005. Explaining Islamophobia: a test of four theories based on a case of a Swiss city. *Swiss Journal of Sociology*, 31(2): 547–66.

Stora, Benjamin. 2021. Les questions mémorielles portant sur la colonisation et la guerre d'Algérie. Rapport, Présidence de la République.

Stovall, Tyler. 1993. Colour-blind France? Colonial workers during the First World War. *Race & Class*, 35(2): 35–55.

Stovall, Tyler. 2006. Race and the making of the nation: Blacks in Modern France. In Michael A. Gomez (ed) *Diasporic Africa: A Reader*, New York; London: New York University Press, pp 200–18.

Taguieff, Pierre-André. 1998. *La couleur et le sang: doctrines racistes à la française.* Paris: Mille et une nuits.

Tevanian, Pierre. 2005. *Le voile médiatique : un faux débat – L'affaire du foulard islamique.* Paris: Editions Raison d'Agir.

Thénault, Sylvie. 2007. L'état d'urgence (1955–2005): de l'algérie coloniale à la france contemporaine; destin d'une loi. *Le Mouvement Social,* 1(218): 63–78.

Thomas, Samuel. 2009. *Le fichage ethno-racial: un outil de discrimination.* Paris: SOS Racisme, Fédération Nationale des Maisons des Potes.

Tin, Louis-Georges. 2008. Who is afraid of Blacks in France? The Black question; the name taboo, the number taboo. *French Politics, Culture & Society,* 26(1): 32–44.

Tobner, Odile. 2007. *Du Racisme Français: quatre siècles de négrophobie.* Paris: Editions des Arènes.

Trench, Brian. 2016. "Charlie Hebdo," Islamophobia, and press freedoms. *Studies: An Irish Quarterly Review,* 105(418): 183–91.

Trica, Danielle. 2006. *Muslim Girls and the Other France: Race, Identity Politics and Social Exclusion.* Bloomington: Indiana University Press.

Tubiana, Michel. 2006. Le silence politique. *Mouvements,* 44(2): 83–7.

Vallot, Pauline. 2016. Petits-enfants d'immigrés face aux études longue: un rapport au système scolaire socialement et historiquement situé. *Revue française de sociologie,* 57(2): 241–68.

Villenave, Baptiste. 2006. La discrimination positive: une présentation; erès. *Vie Sociale,* 3:39–48.

Voltaire. 1734, 1957. *Traité de métaphysique.* Reproduced from the Kehl text. Manchester: Manchester University Press.

Voltaire. 1756, 1759. *An Essay on Universal History, the Manners, and Spirit of Nations, from the Reign of Charlemaign to the Age of Lewis XIV.* London: J. Nourse.

Waddington, David and Mike King. 2012. Contemporary French and British urban riots: an exploration of the underlying political dimensions. In Seraphim Seferiades and Hank Johnston (eds) *Violent Protest, Contentious Politics, and the Neoliberal State,* Farnham: Ashgate, pp 119–32.

Weil, Patrick. 2002. *Qu'est-ce qu'un Français?* Paris: Grasset.

Weil, Patrick. 2005. *La République et sa diversité: immigration, intégration, discriminations.* Paris: Editions du Seuil et la République des Idées.

Wieviorka, Michel. 1998. *Le racisme, une introduction.* Paris: Editions La Découverte.

Wihtol de Wenden, Catherine. 2005. Reflections "a chaud" on the French suburban crisis. Social Science Research Council, November 30.

Williams, Thomas Chatterton. 2019. *Self-Portrait in Black and White: Unlearning Race.* New York: W.W. Norton & Company.

Williams, Thomas Chatterton. 2021. Grand Entretien Eugénie Bastié, *Le Figaro*, February 10.

Wodak, Ruth and Martin Reisigl. 2015. Discourse and racism. In Deborah Tannen, Heidi E. Hamilton, and Deborah Schiffrin (eds) *The Handbook of Discourse Analysis*, 2nd edn, Chichester: Wiley-Blackwell, pp 576–96.

Zauberman, Renée and René Lévy. 1998. La police française et les minorités visibles: les contradictions de l'idéal républicain. In Yves Cartuyvels et al (eds) *Politique, police et justice au bord du futur: mélanges pour et avec Lode Van Outrive*, Paris: L'Harmattan, pp 293–4.

Zirotti, Jean-Pierre. 1989. Constitution d'un domaine de recherche: la scolarisation des enfants de travailleurs immigrés (ETI). *Babylone*, 6-7: 210–54.

Zolberg, Aristide and Litt Woon Long. 1999. Why Islam is like Spanish: cultural incorporation in Europe and the United States. *Politics and Society*, 27: 5–38.

Zompetti, Joseph P. 1997. Toward a Gramscian critical rhetoric. *Western Journal of Communication*, 61(1): 66–86.

Index

References in **bold** type refer to tables.